The **Essential** Buyer's Guide

FORD
MUSTANG

3rd generation 1979 to 1993; inc Mercury Capri 1979 to 1986

T0373726

Your marque expert:
Dave Smith

Veloce's Essential Buyer's Guide
Series
Alfa Romeo Alfasud (Metcalfe)
Alfa Romeo Alfetta: all saloon/sedan models 1972 to 1984 & coupé models 1974 to 1987 (Metcalfe)
Alfa Romeo Giulia GT Coupé (Booker)
Alfa Romeo Giulia Spider (Booker)
Audi TT (Davies)
Audi TT Mk2 2006 to 2014 (Durnan)
Austin-Healey Big Healeys (Trummel)
BMW Boxer Twins (Henshaw)
BMW E30 3 Series 1981 to 1994 (Hosier)
BMW GS (Henshaw)
BMW X5 (Saunders)
BMW Z3 Roadster (Fishwick)
BMW Z4: E85 Roadster and E86 Coupé including M and Alpina 2003 to 2009 (Smitheram)
BSA 350, 441 & 500 Singles (Henshaw)
BSA 500 & 650 Twins (Henshaw)
BSA Bantam (Henshaw)
Choosing, Using & Maintaining Your Electric Bicycle (Henshaw)
Citroën 2CV (Paxton)
Citroën DS & ID (Heilig)
Cobra Replicas (Ayre)
Corvette C2 Sting Ray 1963-1967 (Falconer)
Datsun 240Z 1969 to 1973 (Newlyn)
DeLorean DMC-12 1981 to 1983 (Williams)
Ducati Bevel Twins (Falloon)
Ducati Desmodue Twins (Falloon)
Ducati Desmoquattro Twins – 851, 888, 916, 996, 998, ST4 1988 to 2004 (Falloon)
FIAT 124 Spider & Pininfarina Azzura Spider, (AS-DS) 1966 to 1985 (Robertson)
Fiat 500 & 600 (Bobbitt)
Ford Capri (Paxton)
Ford Escort Mk1 & Mk2 (Williamson)
Ford Focus Mk1 RS & ST170, 1st Generation (Williamson)
Ford Model A – All Models 1927 to 1931 (Buckley)
Ford Model T – All models 1909 to 1927 (Barker)
Ford Mustang – First Generation 1964 to 1973 (Cook)
Ford Mustang – Fifth Generation (2005-2014) (Cook)
Ford RS Cosworth Sierra & Escort (Williamson)
Harley-Davidson Big Twins (Henshaw)
Hillman Imp (Morgan)
Hinckley Triumph triples & fours 750, 900, 955, 1000, 1050, 1200 – 1991-2009 (Henshaw)
Honda CBR FireBlade (Henshaw)
Honda CBR600 Hurricane (Henshaw)
Honda SOHC Fours 1969-1984 (Henshaw)
Jaguar E-Type 3.8 & 4.2 litre (Crespin)
Jaguar E-type V12 5.3 litre (Crespin)
Jaguar Mark 1 & 2 (All models including Daimler 2.5-litre V8) 1955 to 1969 (Thorley)

Jaguar New XK 2005-2014 (Thorley)
Jaguar S-Type – 1999 to 2007 (Thorley)
Jaguar X-Type – 2001 to 2009 (Thorley)
Jaguar XJ-S (Crespin)
Jaguar XJ6, XJ8 & XJR (Thorley)
Jaguar XK 120, 140 & 150 (Thorley)
Jaguar XK8 & XKR (1996-2005) (Thorley)
Jaguar/Daimler XJ 1994-2003 (Crespin)
Jaguar/Daimler XJ40 (Crespin)
Jaguar/Daimler XJ6, XJ12 & Sovereign (Crespin)
Kawasaki Z1 & Z900 (Orritt)
Lancia Delta HF 4WD & Integrale (Baker)
Land Rover Discovery Series 1 (1989-1998) (Taylor)
Land Rover Discovery Series 2 (1998-2004) (Taylor)
Land Rover Series I, II & IIA (Thurman)
Land Rover Series III (Thurman)
Lotus Elan, S1 to Sprint and Plus 2 to Plus 2S 130/5 1962 to 1974 (Vale)
Lotus Europa, S1, S2, Twin-cam & Special 1966 to 1975 (Vale)
Lotus Seven replicas & Caterham 7: 1973-2013 (Hawkins)
Mazda MX-5 Miata (Mk1 1989-97 & Mk2 98-2001) (Crook)
Mazda RX-8 (Parish)
Mercedes-Benz 190: all 190 models (W201 series) 1982 to 1993 (Parish)
Mercedes-Benz 280-560SL & SLC (Bass)
Mercedes-Benz G-Wagen (Greene)
Mercedes-Benz Pagoda 230SL, 250SL & 280SL roadsters & coupés (Bass)
Mercedes-Benz S-Class W126 Series (Zoporowski)
Mercedes-Benz S-Class Second Generation W116 Series (Parish)
Mercedes-Benz SL R129-series 1989 to 2001 (Parish)
Mercedes-Benz SLK (Bass)
Mercedes-Benz W123 (Parish)
Mercedes-Benz W124 – All models 1984-1997 (Zoporowski)
MG Midget & A-H Sprite (Horler)
MG TD, TF & TF1500 (Jones)
MGA 1955-1962 (Crosier)
MGB & MGB GT (Williams)
MGF & MG TF (Hawkins)
Mini (Paxton)
Morgan 4/4 (Benfield)
Morgan Plus 4 (Benfield)
Morris Minor & 1000 (Newell)
Moto Guzzi 2-valve big twins (Falloon)
New Mini (Collins)
Norton Commando (Henshaw)
Peugeot 205 GTI (Blackburn)
Piaggio Scooters – all modern two-stroke & four-stroke automatic models 1991 to 2016 (Willis)
Porsche 356 (Johnson)
Porsche 911 (964) (Streather)
Porsche 911 (991) (Streather)

Porsche 911 (993) (Streather)
Porsche 911 (996) (Streather)
Porsche 911 (997) – Model years 2004 to 2009 (Streather)
Porsche 911 (997) – Second generation models 2009 to 2012 (Streather)
Porsche 911 Carrera 3.2 (Streather)
Porsche 911SC (Streather)
Porsche 924 – All models 1976 to 1988 (Hodgkins)
Porsche 928 (Hemmings)
Porsche 930 Turbo & 911 (930) Turbo (Streather)
Porsche 944 (Higgins)
Porsche 981 Boxster & Cayman (Streather)
Porsche 986 Boxster (Streather)
Porsche 987 Boxster and Cayman 1st generation (2005-2009) (Streather)
Porsche 987 Boxster and Cayman 2nd generation (2009-2012) (Streather)
Range Rover – First Generation models 1970 to 1996 (Taylor)
Range Rover – Second Generation 1994-2001 (Taylor)
Range Rover – Third Generation L322 (2002-2012) (Taylor)
Reliant Scimitar GTE (Payne)
Rolls-Royce Silver Shadow & Bentley T-Series (Bobbitt)
Rover 2000, 2200 & 3500 (Marrocco)
Royal Enfield Bullet (Henshaw)
Subaru Impreza (Hobbs)
Sunbeam Alpine (Barker)
Triumph 350 & 500 Twins (Henshaw)
Triumph Bonneville (Henshaw)
Triumph Herald & Vitesse (Ayre)
Triumph Spitfire and GT6 (Ayre)
Triumph Stag (Mort)
Triumph Thunderbird, Trophy & Tiger (Henshaw)
Triumph TR2 & TR3 – All models (including 3A & 3B) 1953 to 1962 (Conners)
Triumph TR4/4A & TR5/250 – All models 1961 to 1968 (Child & Battyll)
Triumph TR6 (Williams)
Triumph TR7 & TR8 (Williams)
Triumph Trident & BSA Rocket III (Rooke)
TVR Chimaera and Griffith (Kitchen)
TVR S-series (Kitchen)
Velocette 350 & 500 Singles 1946 to 1970 (Henshaw)
Vespa Scooters – Classic two-stroke models 1960-2008 (Paxton)
Volkswagen Bus (Copping)
Volkswagen Transporter T4 (1990-2003) (Copping/Cservenka)
VW Golf GTI (Copping)
VW Beetle (Copping)
Volvo 700/900 Series (Beavis)
Volvo P1800/1800S, E & ES 1961 to 1973 (Murray)

www.veloce.co.uk

First published in April 2022 by Veloce Publishing Limited, Veloce House, Parkway Farm Business Park, Middle Farm Way, Poundbury, Dorchester, Dorset, DT1 3AR, England. Tel 01305 260068/Fax 01305 250479/
e-mail info@veloce.co.uk/web www.veloce.co.uk or www.velocebooks.com.
ISBN: 978-1-787117-30-3. UPC: 6-36847-01730-90
British Library Cataloguing in Publication Data – A catalogue record for this book is available from the British Library.
Typesetting, design and page make-up all by Veloce Publishing Ltd on Apple Mac.
Printed and bound by TJ Books Limited, Padstow, Cornwall.

A 1991 Mustang GT hatchback – a rising star in the classic muscle car world.
(Courtesy Ford Motor Co)

Ever since its introduction in the spring of 1964, Ford's Mustang has had a loyal and passionate following. Now, as the Mustang heads towards its 60th birthday, neither the brand nor the faithful fan club is showing any signs of diminishing.

When the first Mustang debuted in 1964 it was a marketing triumph. Ford managed to take the bargain basement Falcon's running gear, put it in a sexy, sporty suit, and sell it at a price that made stylish motoring available for mundane motor money. More recently, the new-for-2005 S197 model reignited the fading fire under the brand with modern powerplants and styling that harked back to the glory days of 1969. At the time of writing, we have the sixth generation S550, introduced in 2015. It's no longer America's favourite sports coupe; it's the world's favourite.

The Mustang has been in constant production since day one, but, between the 'classics' of 1964-1973 and the performance grand tourers of the 21st century, there were well in excess of five million Mustangs built that have long been under-appreciated. The Mustang II, introduced for the 1974 model year, is a case in point. The 1973 Mustang was a huge, heavy beast with a hood the size of a helipad, and evocatively-named, high-powered, gas-guzzling engines beneath – Boss, Mach I, Super Cobra Jet, etc. The 1974 Mustang was a culture shock. It was

The mighty 1973 Mustang Mach I, the last of the 'classics.' (Courtesy Ford Motor Co)

3

The 1978 Mustang II was much smaller, and still struggles to be seen as a classic, even with the hairy King Cobra package! (Courtesy Ford Motor Co)

tiny by comparison, and there was no V8 engine option. Times had changed, fuel economy and emissions had become an issue, and the OPEC-engineered fuel crisis ended the gas-guzzler's days. The new downsized, small-engined, Pinto-based Mustang II was the right car for the time, and while fans of the hairy-chested pony car wailed over what they saw as a sell-out, Ford sold more Mustangs that year than it had since 1967.

This 1976 design mock-up looks very much like the car that went into production in late 1978. The turbine wheels are interesting, too ... (Courtesy Ford Motor Co)

The third generation of Mustang was introduced in late 1978 as a 1979 model, and set things back on track. It was based on Ford's new 'Fox' platform, first used under the 1978 Ford Fairmont/Mercury Zephyr, but with a shorter wheelbase. The styling was all new, with a European flair, light years away from its three-box Fairmont/Zephyr siblings, and, with a wide range of engines and options, sales soared again. There was a near-identical Mercury version, badged Capri.

The 'Fox' Mustang lived for 15 straight years, a tremendously long life for one platform, with well over 2.5 million sold. In fact, the fourth generation Mustang, introduced for the 1994 model year, used a modified version of the Fox underpinnings right up until 2004.

The Fox Mustang has long been viewed as the poor relation to the classic and

Hard to believe that the stylish Fox was based upon the boxy Fairmont's underpinnings. (Courtesy Ford Motor Co)

The new-for-1994 SN95 Mustang used a modified Fox chassis. This press shot leans heavily on its sixties forebears, and puts the Fox right at the back. (Courtesy Ford Motor Co)

modern Mustangs. Once they became cheap used cars, hot rodders and kit Cobra builders saw V8 Foxes as the disposable box that an engine, transmission and rear end came in.

Now the Fox Mustang is beginning to gain a new legion of fans that are building, restoring, racing and, most importantly, driving these practical, accessible and affordable pony cars. The fact that you're holding this book suggests that you might like to be one of them. Come on in ...

Contents

The Essential Buyer's Guide™ currency

At the time of publication a BG unit of currency "●" equals approximately £1.00/US$1.36/Euro 1.20. Please adjust to suit current exchange rates using Sterling as the base currency.

1 Is it the right car for you?
– marriage guidance

The Fox Mustang came in three body styles: 2dr coupe (commonly called a 'notchback' or 'notch'), 3dr hatchback and 2dr convertible. All Mercury Capris were hatchbacks. All are a whisker under 15ft (4562mm) long and 52in (1318mm) tall, so should fit most domestic garages, but at up to 69in (1755mm) from mirror-to-mirror, and with long doors, watch the width!

All Foxes are four-seaters with no room (or seatbelt) for a third rear passenger. Two adults can sit quite comfortably in the back for shorter journeys, but they'll need to be quite limber to get in and out.

The trunk on the coupe and convertible is small and shallow, with room for a couple of mid-sized suitcases. The hatch is much more capacious, and with the rear seat folded you'll be surprised by how much it can swallow.

I wouldn't recommend a Fox for towing anything more than a small luggage trailer or motorcycle/jet-ski.

The vast majority of Foxes had power-assisted steering and brakes, and are

This is the 1979 coupe, or notchback, body style. (Courtesy Ford Motor Co)

easy to manage. All of the standard engines will happily run on regular unleaded, though none was designed for fuels containing ethanol. Some manual transmissions can take a bit of getting used to, with a heavy clutch and notchy shifter.

The hatchback is a practical proposition with a reasonable capacity for luggage. This is a 1990 LX. (Courtesy Ford Motor Co)

This 1983 example is one of the first convertibles. (Courtesy Ford Motor Co)

The Mercury Capri had nose, tail and trim differences as well as the flared-out wheelarches. This is a 1983 model. (Courtesy Ford Motor Co)

All Foxes are now old enough to enjoy classic/collector policies through specialist insurers, and should be cheap and easy to insure unless it's your daily driver or you're a younger driver.

A Fox Mustang is a usable and practical retro/classic. All will happily trundle around town, and while the V8 is happiest out on the highway, the four- and six-cylinder engines will still keep up with traffic.

2 Cost considerations
– affordable, or a money pit?

A = www.rockauto.com
B = www.npdlink.com
C = www.lmr.com

Basic service – air, oil & fuel filters, sparkplugs (A)
1979 2.3 – from x11.06
1986 3.8 V6 – from x9.68
1990 5.0 V8 – from x13.11

Front brake pads (set of four)
1979 2.3 – from x3.35 (A), branded from x16.98 (B) or x24.99 (C)
1986 3.8 V6 – from x2.46 (A), branded from x33.63 (B) or x29.99 (C)
1990 5.0 V8 – from x3.35 (A), branded x27.55 (B) or x42.99 (C). High-
performance from x112.15 (B) or x76.16 (C)

Front fender, all 1979-1990 Mustang models
Pattern/repro from x39.47 (A), x59.95 (B), x164.99 (C)

Full floorpan, all models
Pattern/repro from x449.99 (B), x399.95 (C)
Half pan from x113 per side (A)

This guide is for standard production Mustang. Parts specific to the Capri may
cost more and be harder to find. Likewise, expect to pay a considerable premium
for parts specific to low-volume models such as SVO or late SVO Cobra models.
Anybody outside North America will have to factor shipping, duties and taxes into
the bottom line.

A Fox, such as this 1982 GT, is a fast-appreciating classic that's still daily drivable.
(Courtesy Ford Motor Co)

At the time of writing, the Fox Mustang and Capri have bottomed out at the 'old beater' stage of their lives, and are rapidly heading up the slope toward classic status. They are also in that sweet spot of being old enough to be called classic or retro, but young enough to still be modern, reliable drivers. This makes them a superb entry to classic ownership for beginners, and a canny investment for seasoned collectors.

Because Ford built millions of cars on the Fox platform, powertrain and running gear parts availability is excellent and prices are very reasonable. Plus, because the Mustang/Capri is (and always has been) a very popular choice for hot street, strip and track car builds, you'll be spoiled for choice with aftermarket upgrades and performance parts.

Outside the US/Canada, if you ask for an oil filter or sparkplugs for a 1989 Ford Mustang 5.0, you might be met with a blank look from the parts counter guy; ask for a Fram PH8A filter or Champion RV15YC4 sparkplugs and they'll probably be on the shelf.

A well-informed amateur with a reasonably well-stocked toolbox can undertake most servicing and basic repair, as there are few special tools required and access is rarely an issue. One headache-inducing idiosyncrasy is that Foxes were built during the prolonged handover from imperial to metric – most of the body/suspension fasteners are metric and most of the engine fasteners are imperial!

Body condition is the most critical aspect of any Fox. An enthusiastic amateur can replace the bolt-on panels – front fenders, doors, hoods, trunk lids/tailgates and

Starting with the most rust-free Fox you can find prevents headaches down the line.

noses/rear bumpers – with new or good secondhand parts, but the bodyshell itself is far more involved, and a rotten, bashed, bent or leaky shell can make the difference between a quick fix-up and a long-term strip-down and rebuild. With the youngest Fox now looking at its 30th birthday, few will have escaped a visit from the tinworm.

Mustang specialists in America are firmly on the Fox's popularity

The basic, carburetted 2.3 Pinto is unlikely to stir a gearhead's emotions, but it's fine for a Sunday drive.

bandwagon, supplying restoration and repair parts, and even reproducing long-obsolete bits, so it seems that the future is rosy.

There were five engines fitted to the Fox Mustang: the 140ci (2301cc) four-cylinder, naturally-aspirated or turbocharged; the 171ci (2792cc) V6; the 200ci

(3277cc) straight six, the 232ci (3797cc) V6, and the 255 or 302ci (4178/4949cc) V8.

The 140ci 'Pinto' overhead-cam four-cylinder was previously used in the Ford Pinto and, although they look very similar, it shares little with the 1.3-2.0 European Pinto engine. The naturally-aspirated version was used through all model years, from the rather weedy 88hp version in 1979 to the slightly stouter twin-plug 105hp version in 1991-on models. There were turbocharged versions, and the early draw-through carburettor versions gave a sprightly 130hp when new, but were unreliable and tricky to tune. The fuel-injected 1983-84 versions were much better, and the intercooled 1984-1986 SVO Mustang was a

The European narrow-angle 2.8-litre Cologne V6 was short-lived – it was dropped after 1979. (Courtesy Ford Motor Co)

200hp treat, though the latter is now in collector car territory.

The 109hp 2.8-litre V6 is a German-built, but Americanised, carburetted version of the European 'Cologne' narrow-angle OHV V6. It was only used in 1979 before demand outstripped supply and Ford had to revert to the elderly 200ci Falcon OHV straight-six – a heavy, plodding motor giving just 89hp, but with a reputation for bulletproof reliability.

The 3.8-litre 'Essex' V6 replaced the old Falcon six for the 1983 model year. Confusingly, it was built in Ford's Essex Engine Plant in Canada, but had nothing to do with the Ford 'Essex' V6 built in Essex, England. This overhead-valve, aluminium-headed, carburetted V6 put out 112hp, but 1984-on models used single-point central fuel-injection to give 120hp until the V6 option was dropped altogether after 1986.

The 302ci Windsor V8 is, of course, the engine everyone wants. At the model's 1979 introduction, V8 models were badged '5.0-Liter' and stayed that way; however, in 1980 and 1981, Ford sneaked in a sleeved-down 255ci version to help pass new smog laws. Externally identical to the 302, the 255 was rather limp-wristed, and is nobody's favourite engine.

As the years went by, the 302 gained central fuel-injection (optional, 1984-1985), roller-lifter camshaft (optional 1985, standard 1986-on), multi-point electronically controlled fuel-injection (standard 1986-on), forged pistons (phased in from 1985, standard from 1987) and other upgrades. The post-1986 V8s are generally seen as the best of the bunch, being reliable and totally drivable, yet with tyre-smoking hooliganism just one throttle-prod away.

This is the early 5.0 in Don Hardy's '79 Mercury Capri ...

If you want a handsome retro/classic for weekend cruises or trips to car shows, any of these engines will be fine, but if you want performance, you'll only be disappointed with anything less than the V8. It's the most desirable and will therefore hold its price better, and there isn't a huge fuel economy price to pay – my 1990 5.0 LX auto would return 30 miles to an imperial gallon at a steady 60mph.

... while this is the fuel-injected 5.0 in his ASC McLaren convertible.

The Fox is unusual in that the convertible doesn't command a price premium over the coupe or hatch. There's nothing wrong with the ragtop, but performance-minded buyers are usually looking for a tintop to take racing, so these fetch the best prices.

At the time of writing you could still find Foxes for around ⬤x1000, but these are likely to be incomplete, damaged or in need of serious remedial work – these are parts cars, or full rebuilds.

For ⬤x2000 you might get a four- or six-cylinder car that's mostly complete and possibly running but in need of some restoration. These might be rolling restorations that you could fix up along the way. Add an extra ⬤x1000 for a V8.

A ⬤x5000 budget could land you a V8 that's ready to drive and enjoy. It won't be perfect, but should be a good, solid base to start from.

The ⬤x10,000+ price tags are reserved for the best production Foxes needing little or nothing but polishing. Concours winners, desirable special editions, and delivery-mileage survivors are already fetching much more than this at high-profile collector car auctions.

Later models are currently more sought-after than early ones, and a 1988-1993 5.0 LX coupe is the Holy Grail for performance fans.

A plain-Jane 1988 LX coupe with a V8 is something of a sleeper, and a great base for a performance street/strip build. (Courtesy Ford Motor Co)

5 Before you view
– be well informed

To avoid a wasted journey, and the disappointment of finding that the car does not match your expectations, it will help if you're very clear about what questions you want to ask before you pick up the telephone. Some of these points might appear basic but when you're excited about the prospect of buying your dream classic, it's amazing how some of the most obvious things slip the mind ...

Where is the car?
Is it going to be worth travelling to the next county/state or even across a border? A locally-advertised car, although it may not sound very interesting, can add to your knowledge for very little effort, so make a visit – it might even be in better condition than expected.

Dealer or private sale?
Establish early on if the car is being sold by its owner or by a trader. A private owner should have all the history, so don't be afraid to ask detailed questions. A dealer may have limited knowledge of a car's history but should have some documentation. A dealer may offer a warranty/guarantee (ask for a printed copy) and finance.

Cost of collection and delivery?
A dealer may well be used to quoting for delivery by car transporter. A private owner may agree to meet you halfway, but only agree to this after you have seen the car at the vendor's address to validate the documents. Conversely, you could meet halfway and agree the sale but insist on meeting at the vendor's address for the handover.

View – when and where?
It is always preferable to view at the vendor's home or business premises. In the case of a private sale, the car's documentation should tally with the vendor's name and address. Arrange to view only in daylight and avoid a wet day. Most cars look better in poor light or when wet.

Reason for sale?
Do make it one of the first questions. Why is the car being sold and how long has it been with the current owner? How many previous owners?

Left-hand to right-hand drive?
No Fox was factory-built right-hand drive, so any conversion is third-party. In the UK, Ford imported new early Foxes to be converted by a third-party company and sold new through selected Ford dealers. It was a short-lived venture; few were sold, and few remain. While the work itself was good quality, the fact that Fox engines are offset towards the passenger side of the bay meant that conversion was a series of compromises – it was tricky on a four- or six-cylinder car, and damn near impossible on a V8. Unless your local or national laws demand it, don't even consider LHD-to-RHD conversion. A RHD conversion doesn't make a Fox more valuable, and usually

This is Lee Reed's 1982 GLX 3.3 straight six, converted to RHD from new. Such conversions are available through a handful of Ford dealerships in the UK. (Courtesy Lee Reed)

makes it worth less, despite its rarity. I've seen ads from sellers convinced that RHD doubles the car's value. It doesn't. Don't pay extra for their delusion.

Condition (body/chassis/interior/mechanicals)?
Ask for an honest appraisal of the car's condition. Ask specifically about some of the check items described in chapter 7.

All original specification?
Do you want an all-original car for restoration, or a stripped-out, modified street/strip road-burner? There's no sense in settling for one when you really want the other.

Matching data/legal ownership?
Do VIN/chassis, engine numbers and licence plate match the official registration documents? Is the owner's name and address recorded correctly in those documents?

For those countries that require an annual roadworthiness test, does the car have a document showing that it complies? In the UK, MOT certificates can be verified online.

If a smog/emissions certificate is mandatory, does the car have one?

If required, does the car carry a current road fund licence/licence plate tag? Does the vendor own the car outright? Money might be owed to a bank or finance

company; the car could even be stolen. Several organisations will supply the ownership data based on the car's licence plate number, for a fee. Such companies can often also tell you whether the car has been written-off by an insurance company. In the UK, these companies can supply vehicle data:
HPI – 01722 422 422
AA – 0870 600 0836
DVLA – 0870 240 0010
RAC – 0870 533 3660
Other countries will have similar organisations.

Unleaded fuel?
All Foxes were built to run on regular unleaded fuel, though none were built to cope with fuel containing ethanol.

Insurance?
Check with your existing insurer before setting out, your current policy might not cover you to drive the car if you do purchase it.

How you can pay?
A cheque/check will take several days to clear, and the seller may prefer to sell to a cash buyer. A banker's draft (a cheque issued by a bank) is as good as cash but safer, so contact your bank and familiarise yourself with the formalities necessary to obtain one.

Buying at auction?
See chapter 10 for further advice.

Professional vehicle checks?
There are often marque/model specialists who will undertake professional examination of a vehicle on your behalf. Owners' clubs may be able to put you in touch with a specialist. Other organisations that will carry out a general professional check in the UK are:
AA – 0800 085 3007 (motoring organisation with vehicle inspectors)
ABS – 0800 358 5855 (specialist vehicle inspection company)
RAC – 0870 533 3660 (motoring organisation with vehicle inspectors)
Other countries will have similar organisations

6 Inspection equipment
– these items will really help

This book
Reading glasses (if you need them for close work)
Magnet (not powerful; a fridge magnet is ideal)
Flashlight
Probe (a small screwdriver works well)
Overalls
Mirror on a stick
Digital camera/smartphone
A friend, preferably a knowledgeable enthusiast

Before you rush out of the door, gather together a few items that will help as you work your way around the car. This book is designed to be your guide at every step, so take it along and use the check boxes to help you assess each area of the car you're interested in. Don't be afraid to let the seller see you using it.

Take your reading glasses if you need them to read documents and make close-up inspections.

A magnet will help you check if the car is full of filler or has fibreglass panels. Use it to sample bodywork areas all around the car but take care not to damage the paint. Expect to find a little filler here and there, but not whole panels. There's nothing wrong with fibreglass panels, but a purist might want the car to be as original as possible.

A flashlight with fresh batteries, or the light on your smartphone, will be useful for peering into the wheelarches and under the car.

A small screwdriver can be used (with care) as a probe, particularly in the wheelarches and underside. With this you should be able to check areas of corrosion, but be careful – it it's really bad, the screwdriver could go straight through the metal!

Be prepared to get dirty – take along a pair of overalls if you have them. Fixing a mirror at an angle on the end of a stick may seem odd, but will help you check the condition of the underside of the car and help peer into nooks, crannies and crevices. You can also use it, with the flashlight, along the underside of the sills/rockers and on the floors.

If you have the use of a digital camera/smartphone, take it along so that later you can study some areas of the car more closely. Take a picture of any part of the car that causes you concern and seek a friend's opinion.

Ideally, have a friend or knowledgeable enthusiast accompany you. A second opinion is always valuable and can help stop you getting carried away!

So, you're looking for the Fox to suit you perfectly. You've looked in the usual places – eBay, craigslist, Facebook Marketplace, local newspaper small ads, magazine classifieds, Fox fan forums, club sites and Facebook pages – and you've found a promising lead. It's time to give the suspect a quick once-over. Have you also considered going to local classic car shows or drag strips and looking for Foxes with a 'For Sale' sign in the window? You could give the car a quick inspection right there and then if the owner is agreeable.

The best item you can have in your arsenal is a good friend. If you really want to own a car like this, then the first sight of it could allow your emotions to take over,

The dream – "1989 Mustang GT hatch, one enthusiast owner from new, low miles, perfect condition but ashtray's full, hence $1000." (Courtesy Ford Motor Co)

The reality – "1987 Mustang GT hatch, been thrashed by everyone who got behind the wheel then stored in knee-deep mud for five years, but hey, don't lowball me, I know what I got ..."

and the part of your brain that's already smitten at the sight of a Mustang can blind you to the fact that the car you're looking at is actually nothing but a rusty pit of pain for you to shovel time and money into. That good friend can act as a lightning rod for your over-enthusiasm and prevent you reaching for your wallet while your brain is making 'vroom, vroom' noises.

First, stand back and take a good look at the car from a distance. Does it sit right? Are there any signs of sagging suspension, or even something more serious, making it lean to one side or nose up/down?

Now get close up and take a good look along the length of the car on each side. The production line workers at Dearborn were very good at assembling Fox Mustangs quickly, but they didn't waste too much time on panel gap perfection; however, none should have gaps tight enough to scuff the paint off adjacent panels or wide enough to fit a pencil between. These would suggest amateur panel replacement or accident damage repair.

Can you see any rust anywhere? Every square inch of rust you can see usually has at least three friends hiding nearby. Beware of statements in adverts along

What you want – "1981 Mercury Capri, delivery miles only, wrapped in cotton wool then dry stored since new." (Courtesy Ford Motor Co)

the lines of "surface rust only" – rust doesn't work like that. Steel has a 'grain,' like wood, and rust doesn't sit on the surface like a tablecloth on a table; it works its way into the steel. There's also a world of difference between the beautiful, sun-baked desert 'patina' rust on an Arizona car and the horrible, flaky, crumbling rust on a salt-belt car.

Check over the paintwork. There's a guide to common paint problems in chapter 14, but you're also looking for aging and matching. Is it the original colour? If you can find the paint code on the door tag you can Google it. Again, Ford wasn't striving for paint perfection on the production line back then, and generally the factory finish on later Foxes was better than that on early cars. Is the paint colour consistent, or does it vary from panel to panel, which could indicate that extensive repairs have been carried out? There's a huge gulf of difference between a professional bodyshop spending weeks preparing a car for a masterpiece paint job and someone blowing on a quick coat on using rattle cans on his/her driveway one Sunday. Has any paintwork been done very, very recently? It could be covering fresh, professional repairs, or covering up a whole drum of Bondo/body filler.

Pop the hood – the release handle is beneath the steering column. Is the engine warm? If the owner has just got home from work, fair enough, but otherwise this could suggest that he/she has warmed up the engine prior to your arrival, perhaps to hide cold-starting issues.

What you get – "1990 Mustang LX, never raced or rallied ..." (Courtesy Martin Drake)

Take a good look around the engine and engine bay. Is it dirty or rusty? Dirt washes off; rust doesn't. Does the wiring look original, or has it been messed with, and if so, why? If the owner has parked the car in its usual spot, look for tell-tale oil stains on the ground.

Dip the oil – does it look fresh and golden, or is it like tar? Likewise, dip the auto transmission fluid – it should be clear blood red and smell sweet; if it's brown and smells burnt, beware. Check the power steering reservoir – the dipstick is attached to the cap. This fluid should also be red and sweet smelling. If the engine is cool, remove the coolant overflow tank cap – early models have this attached to the left-hand inner fender; later models have it mounted to the radiator's fan shroud. Is there nice, clean coolant in there, or rusty sludge? Is there any brown/white mayonnaise around the cap? This would indicate oil getting into the water, and that's never good.

Close the hood by lowering it most of the way, then dropping it the last two or three inches. Does it close securely, flush with the surrounding bodywork, and without needing you to jump on it to get it to latch?

Next, look in the trunk. Check the weatherstrip around the opening, and the corners just above the taillights, a common rust trap on coupes and convertibles. Is the trunk dry, or does it look/smell damp? If there's water getting in there, you'll need to find out how. Use a flashlight to look inside the drop-offs into the lower quarters behind the rear wheel wells. What's down there – solid steel, water, rust, filler, crud or daylight? When you shut the trunk, does it latch flush and secure? Hatchbacks are the worst offenders for trunks that don't shut as well as they should.

Now we need to open the doors. First off, do they open and shut properly? The Foxes have long doors with heavy built-in crash protection beams, all supported by two little hinges, so check for wear and dropping. The driver's door obviously gets used more than the passenger door, so check that first.

Now check the carpets. Are they damp, or do they smell damp and musty? If the car has been stored somewhere bone-dry for a length of time, the carpets may be dry, but that smell will hang around. Try pouring a bottle of water over the base of the windshield and down into the cowl vent behind the wipers. If the carpet suddenly gets damp, there's trouble in store. On the other hand, if the owner has gone to the trouble of dry-storing the car, he/she may not appreciate you soaking it!

Check the headlining the same way. If the car has a sunroof, they can leak and soak the back of the headlining. If there's a leak in the cowl, water gets in, evaporates, then condenses on the front of the headlining. Yes, the damp gets to it coming *and* going …

Take a general look around the interior. Does the overall wear and tear on the upholstery, pedal pads and steering wheel match the mileage on the odometer? Is the dash top baked and split? Has the original radio been replaced with an aftermarket unit, and, if so, has it been done carefully and properly or has it been hacked into the dash/console with a spade? Check any other accessories, gauges and so on, and the wiring that goes with them.

Right, you've spent ten minutes poking around the car, you've earned a rest, so get a piece of carpet or cardboard and have a lie-down. While you're down there, look under the car with your flashlight. You'll never get the full picture without having the car on a ramp or lift, but at least check for anything hanging down that shouldn't, or rust in the rockers or floors.

Is the underside of the car covered in oil? This would suggest serious leakage. Or has it been liberally coated in fresh underbody sealer? Underseal is good to have, but not if it's there to hide anything from poor repairs to rusted brake pipes.

Check the tyres and wheels. Are the wheels original or aftermarket, and are they a suitable size and offset or are there marks where they've rubbed the bodywork or chassis on full steering lock? Are the tyres a good brand, with the correct speed rating and a matching set on all four corners? Or are they cheap retreads with age-crazing and that tell-tale line of cracks in the sidewall that suggests they've been flat for years until five minutes before you turned up?

Next, you need to have a good talk with the owner, and the best tool you can use here is a little respect. A Fox Mustang may not be in the same league as a '67 Shelby, but whether the car you're looking at is a perfect survivor, a concours restoration, a barn-find treasure or a complete wreck, it could have a great deal of sentimental value to the owner. It could be his/her pride and joy.

If the owner realises that you're an enthusiast who is going to restore and cherish that pride and joy, he/she is likely to be a lot more forthcoming and honest, and, buy it or not, you could make a friend for life. If he/she thinks that you're just there to kick the tyres, poke holes in it, then joyride it around before telling him/her that it's junk and making an insulting lowball offer, don't expect an invitation to stay for dinner …

Get as much information on the history of the vehicle as you can. Where has it lived its life? Just because it's for sale in California today doesn't mean it hasn't spent the last 30 years in the salt-strewn north-eastern USA. Likewise, if you're looking at buying a base, four-cylinder convertible from its second owner in Florida, the first owner could well have been Hertz or Avis ...

If you're outside North America, find out when the car was exported, and why. Some were private exports, some with owners in the military posted overseas, but some could have been written-off in America, poorly repaired, then exported and registered as plain ol' used cars abroad. A Carfax report may cost a few ● but could save a lot of heartache.

If the opportunity is there, go for a test drive. First, is the car road legal and roadworthy? They don't automatically mean the same thing. Second, if you're expecting to drive the car, show the owner evidence that you're insured to drive a car that you don't own on public roads. If he/she says that you will be covered on his/her policy, or if they have motor traders' blanket cover, ask to see evidence of this.

Turn the key to the 'ign' position, and the dash will light up. The 'check engine' light should also light up, then go out after a second or two; likewise the 'Airbag' light on 1990-on models. If they don't go out, there could be an issue that means it's unwise to drive the car. If they don't light up at all, the bulb could have blown or, more significantly, been removed to hide a major fault.

Before starting the engine, press the brake pedal twice. The first press should feel quite firm, and definitely not go past halfway without a fight. The second press should feel very firm almost immediately and go hardly anywhere. If the pedal sinks with little resistance, abort the mission.

If all is well, and the gauge shows fuel in the tank, start the car. It's worth asking the owner if there's a trick to starting – some carburetted cars might need a pump on the gas pedal before starting; others prefer being left alone. Automatic cars should be in 'P' or 'N,' and manual cars should be in neutral and have the clutch pressed down before the starter will work. If the owner reels off a whole list of jobs you have to do just to get the car started, be very wary.

Does the starter engage smoothly and spin quickly? Does the engine fire almost immediately or after just a second or two? Watch for smoke signals from the tailpipe. Check that the oil pressure light goes out quickly, and/or the oil pressure gauge shows good pressure, and that the battery charging light goes straight out.

Does the engine idle smoothly, or is it coughing and misfiring? The exhaust may smell a little 'rich' from cold start, but if the smell of fuel is making your eyes water, that's not right. Drop the auto shifter into 'D' – does drive engage almost immediately? Anything more than a second suggests low fluid or a tired transmission. Release the parking brake, move away, and listen for the slight 'clunk' of sticking brakes shocking themselves free.

Use your ears. Listen for ticking, tapping or knocking from the engine, blowing from the exhaust, squealing from the fan belt, whining from the transmission or rear end, grumbling from wheel bearings or grinding from the brakes. If the car's been sitting for a while, a little initial noise is acceptable as the brakes clean themselves. How does the steering feel? The Fox rack-and-pinion should feel taut and precise, with little lost motion. Is the car tracking straight, or pulling to one side? That could indicate poor alignment or worn suspension bushes or joints.

On a clear stretch, accelerate. Does the engine stumble or hesitate? Does the auto transmission kickdown a gear cleanly? Does the rear end try to 'steer' the car? Build up some speed, then, if safe to do so, brake firmly. Does the pedal push back and the car shake? That could mean warped rotors. Does the car dive left or right? That could mean a seized calliper.

Check the dashboard. Have any warning lights appeared? Is the temperature gauge showing warm or hot? Is the speedometer reading as you'd expect, or is the needle jumping up and down? Try all the lights, wipers, power windows and other accessories.

How does the car 'feel' overall to you? Tight and sound, or loose and rattly? A little scuttle-shake is to be expected in a convertible, but if it's detaching your retinas then there's something wrong ... Most importantly, how comfortable do you feel in the driver's seat? What does your gut tell you? If your instincts say no, then thank the owner for his/her time and trouble and walk away – there'll be another Fox out there for you. If you feel like you belong there, then it's time for a more serious inspection – move onto the next chapters!

8 Key points
– where to look for problems

The main **VIN** tag is at the base of the windshield (top). If it's not, start worrying.

VIN
The VIN, or chassis number, is stamped onto a plate attached to the cowl and visible through the windshield on the driver's side. Early (1979-1980) cars had an 11-digit VIN; 1981-on cars had 17 digits, and decoding it using online tools can tell you a lot about the car. The VIN may also appear on little stickers dotted around the body on 1988-on cars – do they match the VIN plate?

Door pillar stickers
The VIN, along with various other useful details, also appears on a Vehicle Certification Label in the driver's door area; sometimes on the B-pillar, sometimes on the door itself. Take a photo of it. If it's missing, or been painted over, that could

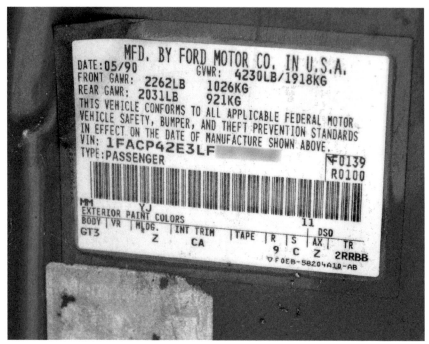

This sticker is on the driver's door – if it doesn't match the main **VIN** plate, it could be a replacement door.

indicate major (or clumsy) repair work. If it's on the door but doesn't match the main VIN, perhaps it's a secondhand door.

Keys
Foxes used one key for the door and trunk locks, and another for the ignition lock. Over the years, keys become more fragile, so if the car comes with only one set of keys, make duplicates right away. Foxes, like many cars of the period, are pitifully easy to break into so any security upgrades are welcome, but beware of cheap, temperamental aftermarket alarms.

Mileage
The odometer only reads to five whole digits, so unless it has provenance to back it up, that '30,000-mile car' could be a 130,000-mile car or even 230,000!

9 Serious evaluation
– 60 minutes for years of enjoyment

Score each section using the boxes as follows:
4 = excellent; 3 = good; 2 = average; 1 = poor. The totting up procedure is detailed at the end of the chapter. Be realistic in your marking!

A garage lift makes an inspection a breeze. If you can use one, do so ...

You've found a Fox and think it could be the one for you – time for a serious inspection. It'll take time and you'll get dirty, so be ready. A two-post or four-post lift would make this job 100% easier, so if the seller has one, use it. If not, perhaps a friendly local mechanic or tyre/exhaust shop might loan you theirs at lunchtime for a couple of banknotes. Failing that, you're going to need a trolley jack and axle stands, and be prepared for crud to fall in your face ...

Roof [4] [3] [2] [1]
Start at the top with one of the most important aspects of any Fox purchase – choose a-e as appropriate.

    a. Convertible Mustang convertibles were made from

Convertible tops don't last forever ... Always check for quality over newness.

1983 onward and began life as coupes, taken off the Dearborn production line and shipped to Cars & Concepts for conversion. An electric motor drives a hydraulic pump and rams to raise and lower the roof, which latches manually to the header rail behind each sunvisor. Does it raise and lower smoothly and evenly on both sides? Does it latch easily, or do you have to fight it? On cold days, the fabric will be stretched tight, but in the sunshine it should be pliant and fold easily without being baggy. With the roof up, check for rips, fraying, patching and discolouration. Replacement top fabric is available and not too expensive, though you get what you pay for, and fitting is not a job for amateurs unless you're very skilled and patient.

b. T-tops This option was available from 1981-1988, almost exclusively fitted to hatchbacks. They looked cool and were great for letting sunshine in, but often let rain in too ... whether the panels were on or off. Do the panels latch securely in place, and is the weatherstripping good? Ten seconds with a hosepipe will tell you how leaky they are, and new weatherstripping is neither cheap nor easy to change. If it's an aftermarket T-top conversion, not factory-fitted, research before you commit. T-tops may be sought after by restorers wanting eighties chic, but performance builders choose solid roof cars for rigidity.

Full vinyl roof and wire wheel trims, this Ghia Coupe was stylish in 1981. (Courtesy Ford Motor Co)

c. Vinyl roof A vinyl roof was optional on hatches and coupes from the start. Ghia models also had a 'carriage roof' option, covering just the back half of the roof and sail panels. Both died out early in the eighties, as it was seen as rather seventies kitsch. If moisture has got under the fabric, the roof rusts away out of sight for years, so look for bubbles under the vinyl – if it goes 'crunch' when you press it, be very wary. Retrofitted vinyl can hide anything, so if it has a non-factory vinyl roof, ask why.

d. Sunroof All hatches and pre-1985 coupes had a sunroof option. It's a glass panel that lifts up at the trailing edge, or, by disconnecting the latch, lifts out altogether. They're secured at the front edge by two metal tangs that slide into plastic receivers in the roof – these tangs rust away unseen, so pop out the sunroof and check. The weatherstrip around the glass panel takes the weather's full force, so look for perishing. There were also companies all over the world that would supply and fit an aftermarket sunroof to a solid roof car ...

e. Solid roof Hatchbacks and coupes without T-tops, sunroof or vinyl are favoured amongst performance builders for greater structural integrity, lighter weight,

Here's a sunroof with perished weather sealing AND rust bubbles in the surrounding metal. Neither is a good sign.

and fewer leaks. The roof panel is one thin steel pressing from front to back and side to side, so rust or damage is tricky to repair, and clumsy welding can warp the whole thing. On hatchbacks, the edge where the roof panel folds into the tailgate aperture is a condensation trap and rusts from the inside.

Pillars

Check all pillars for rust, right into the drip rails. The roof to sail panel joint was lead-loaded at the factory, and rust in the join will be tricky to repair. Convertible and T-top A-pillars and windshield frames had bolt-in reinforcements for rollover protection, so they're structurally crucial and rust/damage is significant.

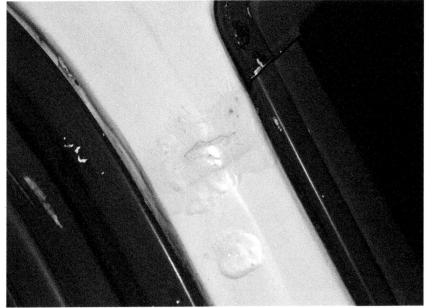

Bubbling where the roof panel joins the pillars could spell trouble.

Windshield 4 3 2 1

Foxes have bonded-in laminated windshields with optional top-tint (the top few inches tinted to reduce sun glare). Check carefully for cracks, stone-chip bullseyes, and scratches from worn-out wipers. A milky, cloudy appearance means delamination – water getting between the glass laminates – and usually begins in the corners, pointing to rust in the adjacent metal. Check the surround trim and look for excess sealant that people apply in a (misguided) attempt to cure water leaks inside the car. The chances of removing a Fox windshield without breaking it are slim, so don't count on finding one secondhand, and, unless you're very confident, fitting is a job for professionals.

Glass 4 3 2 1

Check the door glass for scratches caused by trapped grit or worn-out seals on the doors, and that they raise

Cloudy corners means delamination, and rust in the screen surround.

This patchiness on later models' rear quarter window surrounds is only a problem in aesthetic terms.

and lower smoothly and easily. Rear quarter windows are fixed on the hatch and notch, but the soft plastic surrounds on post-1986 models get a patchy, textured finish. It's not pretty but not critical, so learn to live with it or pay plenty for repro or reconditioned units. Hatch/notch rear screens are bonded in, and 1983-1986 Capris used a distinctive 'bubble' convex screen. Check that convertibles' quarter windows raise and lower smoothly and sit securely in the 'up' position. Many ragtops have a glass rear screen; budget replacement tops use a plastic screen, so check that it's clear and not creased or cloudy.

Tailgate/trunk lid
Both can harbour rust, usually in the corners above the taillights. Hatchbacks use gas struts to keep the tailgate open, and their failure can prove painful ... A hatchback rear screen wiper is a rare option. Check that the tailgate latches shut easily. The notch and convertible use a similar-looking deck lid, but the notch has hinges and torsion springs inside, under the parcel shelf, while the convertible uses external hinges.

Convertibles often have these riveted-on slats for additional carrying capacity.

Hood
1979-1982, 1983-1984, 1985-1986, and 1987-1993 hoods/bonnets are all different and not interchangeable. Check inside and out for rust, starting in the seams at the edges, and for stone chips on the leading edge, especially on 1987-on models. Is the sound-deadening pad still attached to the inside? Early models often used scoops (usually just decorative) – are these present and correct? Matt black decals will fade to grey over the years.

Earlier models often wore scoops and sculpture on the hood; none more so than this 1982 Mercury Capri RS. (Courtesy Ford Motor Co)

Doors

Hatch and notch doors have frames around the glass; convertibles and T-tops use frameless doors, the glass sealing to weatherstrips on the roof and pillars. Fox doors are long, and side-impact protection beams inside make them heavy – do they open and close smoothly and easily? Drooping could be caused by worn hinge pins or worse – see next paragraph. Check for rust or Bondo/body filler, front, back and underneath. Lower repair panels are available.

If the horizontal pressing in the door doesn't line up with the fender and rear quarter, the door is dropping.

Hinge panel ④ ③ ② ①

Use your flashlight to check the pillar where the door hinges attach, and be thorough. It's a great rust trap, letting the tinworm work in peace and privacy until, one day, your doors start drooping ... It's a structurally critical area, and repairs require door and fender removal, at least.

Handles, locks and latches ④ ③ ② ①

Do the door handles feel loose and rattly with lots of lost motion? Have they been used to lift a drooping door onto its latch? Replacement isn't expensive. Door and trunk locks share a key – if the car has different keys for each lock, ask why. If the car has central locking or remote trunk release, check they work properly. The latch pins use a nylon sleeve for the latches to grab onto. If this is damaged or missing, the doors/trunk will never shut properly.

The hinge panel takes lots of abuse, and just loves to rust away out of sight.

If the door locks are stiff to turn with the key, suspect seized central locking solenoids.

The plastic tube onto which the latch grabs is often damaged or even missing, so the door/trunk will not shut properly.

4 3 2 1

Front fenders

The 1979-1990 models use essentially the same fender, while later models have a wider opening for bigger wheels, and all attract rust, accident damage and supermarket cart dings. Check for rust and Bondo, especially in the lower edges, front and rear, and behind plastic mouldings. There should be a plastic wheel well liner; if it's missing, ask why. Cheap repro panels rarely fit well without a lot of work, and Capri fenders are completely different and harder to find.

The top of the right-hand fender usually has the antenna mount, which can be a rust trap.

4 3 2 1

Nose/grille

Foxes use a flexible moulded urethane nose over a bulky bumper bar on impact-absorbing struts. The bar is usually a heavy steel girder, though some very early models used aluminium, while late models used nylon. The nose is designed to shrug off light impact damage, but anything more serious will be harder to repair, especially if the urethane

This GT nose had a nylon bumper bar, much lighter than the steel one.

is ripped. It also needs flexible paint, otherwise it'll crack and peel. Check spoilers low down for road debris or clumsy parking damage; GT fog lamps are also very damage-prone.

Headlights

All 1979-1986 models used four square headlights, hence 'four-eye' Foxes. The earliest cars used sealed-beam units while the rest used halogen bulb units, which give more light, but if the silver inside has corroded they'll need replacing. Higher-wattage bulbs will quickly burn out the headlight switch. SVO models used a unique lamp arrangement, replacements for some of which are rare and very expensive.

Plastic lenses degrade and go cloudy. You can polish them, but some are past saving.

The 1987-1993 'Aero' cars used a trio of flush-fitting lamps. The main headlamp's plastic lens goes cloudy and dull over time, but there are polishing kits on the market to restore clarity. Beware of cheap eBay single-piece headlamp kits, which can be more trouble than they're worth.

Side trims ④ ③ ② ①
Many Foxes had ABS plastic lower body side trims, while Cobras and GTs had deep skirts and trims halfway up the arches, sometimes in a contrasting colour. All suffer debris damage and stonechips, but most problems arise from them being removed then haphazardly refitted, so check for cracks, warping, and odd fasteners. They're also great at concealing rust, so look carefully. Many Foxes also had front-to-rear rubber-coated aluminium rubbing strips glued halfway up the body

No matter how careful you are, you're likely to warp these glued-on trims if you try to remove them.

and, unless you're scrupulously careful, removing them causes them to warp so

The lower quarter behind the wheel takes all the abuse. This one was so rusty you could have poked your finger through it.

they'll never refit properly. Look for twisted or curling strips, and strips that don't line up between panels.

Rear quarters/arches

The rear quarters from doors to taillamps are large, complex and accident-prone panels. Check for rust and filler all over, especially in the lower leading edge where it meets the rocker panel, and the rear lower edge that catches everything the rear wheels throw up. Check the arch lip, plus the rear quarter window recesses and the

This GT bumper cover has been (quite neatly) butchered to take LX exhaust tips.

join between sail panel and roof on hatches and notches. Check behind the fuel filler door in the right-hand quarter. Replacement quarters are available, but they're an involved and skilled job to replace. Capri quarters are different and rare, so expect to pay more.

Rear bumper

The rear bumper is a urethane skin over a steel or nylon crash bar. It's fairly hardy but, like the nose, years and UV damage take their toll. A thin steel strip with studs attached secures the top edge of the bumper skin to the rear panel beneath the taillights, and this can disintegrate through rust. Check the lower edge, too, as many a deep GT bumper has been hacked to clear LX-style tailpipes.

Rear lamps

All Mustang taillamps are a single unit on each side. Early models had six vertical segments, and replacements/reproductions are hard to find. From 1983-1986, they switched to a cleaner, horizontally divided design with amber turn signals. From 1987-1993, the LX used a smart, three-segment version of the '83-'86 unit, while the GT reverted to red turn signals, all hidden behind a plastic 'cheese grater' grille. All are interchangeable with a little work should your country require amber turn signals. Capri taillights are rare.

From 1987, the GT used these 'cheese grater' louvres over the rear lights.

Wipers

The wiper system is generally reliable, with most cars using a two-speed-plus-intermittent arrangement. Blades are standard 16in items, cheap at most auto stores. Check for condition, noise and self-parking.

Cowl/bulkhead

This is probably the most crucial part of a Fox, the difference between a viable project car and the junkyard, or a pleasant driving experience and a giant PITA. The cowl panel, between hood and windshield, supports the wiper spindles and a grille that lets air into the hollow 'balloon' section beneath. That balloon houses the wiper linkage and, at each end, the cabin fresh air vents, with minimal factory rustproofing. The grille lets in air, but also lets in rainwater, leaves, dirt, crud, dead insects, etc, and if all that detritus blocks the drain channels above the door hinge panels, rust sets in, completely out of sight. Even a pinhole in the balloon will give you damp carpets, and even an otherwise rust-free car is likely to have some corrosion in here.

Don Hardy shows the only proper way to seek and destroy rust in the upper cowl section.

This grille lets in almost everything – look at all the leaves in there!

To even begin to cure the symptoms is a major dashboard-out job; to do it 100% properly involves removing the windshield, hood and fenders and drilling dozens of spot-welds. Check this area carefully and patiently – get down in the footwells with your flashlight and watch for leaks while your assistant pours water through the cowl grille. Be wary of cars with steamed-up windows when it hasn't rained all day.

Engine bay

Next, pop the hood. Is it the right engine for the car? This is only important if you're seeking originality; otherwise, there are few performance engines that have never been dropped into Foxes.

Let's assume it's the car's stock engine. Is it the original engine? Does it look clean and cared for, filthy and neglected, or suspiciously clean as though it was

Plenty of bolt-on speed parts on this 347-cube stroker 5.0.

power-washed just before you arrived? Has it been modified? Is there evidence of oil or coolant leakage?

Carburettor/injection

All Foxes had carburettors in 1979. In the mid-eighties, they began switching to electronic fuel-injection with central fuel-injection, a single-point EFI disguised as a carburettor. Nobody loves CFI, and some cars may have been retrofitted with a carb. Likewise, early V8s may have had their two-barrel carbs swapped for an aftermarket four-barrel. If so, has the carburettor been properly fitted, tuned and jetted, or just thrown on straight out of the box? Good carb tuners are a dying breed, so ask around for recommendations.

Beginning in 1986, V8s got the new EEC-IV controlled 'speed-density' sequential fuel-injection that used a manifold absolute pressure (MAP) sensor to measure intake vacuum. In the 1988 model year, they began switching to the 'mass air' system, which uses a mass airflow sensor (MAF) in the pipe between air filter and throttle body – this is the easiest external clue to spot which system you have. The post-1988 225bhp MAF engine is the most sought-after and reliable all-rounder.

Adam Fawlk's 1989 LX doesn't have a MAF because it's running an aftermarket ECU, most of which prefer to use a MAP.

Emissions equipment

Foxes were born in an era when new emissions laws were being passed faster than Detroit could make engines meet them, so all have plenty of smog equipment – AIR pumps, EGR systems, evaporative canisters, etc. The redneck approach is to rip it all off, as if that'd turn the engine into a 1969-spec 400hp tyre-fryer. Wrong. Junking all the emissions gear is unlikely to make it run better; chances are it'll make it worse, and you'll be chasing vacuum leaks and wondering why the 'check engine' light is always on. Check it's all present and correct. Seized Thermactor 'smog pumps' will overheat and kill your catalytic converter.

Alternator

Early Foxes used Motorcraft's 1G 65-amp alternator with external voltage regulator; from 1986, all had the Motorcraft 2G 65- or 75-amp internally regulated unit. All are reliable and cheap to replace, but later EFI models with plenty of accessories will tax a 2G to its limit. Plus, the three-wire multiplug on top of a 2G corrodes, causing high resistance and, in extreme cases, an electrical fire. The more powerful 1994 Mustang 3G alternator is a simple upgrade.

4 3 2 1
Starter

Most Foxes used a broadly similar starter until the very latest nineties models, which used lighter PMGR (Permanent Magnet Gear Reduction) units. New or remanufactured units are available and reasonably priced. Many starter problems can be traced to the remote-mounted starter solenoid. If this fails, replace it with Motorcraft or another good brand; avoid no-name far-Eastern parts.

4 3 2 1
Ignition system

All Foxes used distributors until the very last 2.3-litre models, which used an EDIS distributorless system. Early models used Ford's Duraspark ignition modules, switching to the distributor-mounted Thick Film Integrated (TFI) module when fuel-injection took over from 1984. Both are generally reliable, though overheated TFI modules

The later V8 distributor with TFI module mounted on the side.

can cause strange starting and running problems. Earlier models used a standard canister coil; later fuel-injected models used a specific coil mounted to the left inner fender. Check the distributor cap and rotor for burning and tracking, and the plug leads for fit and match.

Fuel system

4 3 2 1

Carburetted Foxes have a mechanical fuel pump mounted to the engine; EFI models have an electric pump in or near the tank. All will have flexible rubber pipes and unions in the system, which won't be ethanol fuel compatible, so look hard for possible leaks. If the car's been sitting a long time, take a sniff at the filler cap or carburettor. Stale gasoline stinks, and if you smell stale fuel, don't even crank the engine – it will drag rust and sediment up from the tank.

Serpentine belts run some accessories – in this case, the water pump – 'backwards' from the non-ribbed side of the belt. Adam's engine has had a Thermactor delete ...

Fan belt(s)
Earlier cars used traditional V-belts; later cars and all V8s used the flat, ribbed belt on 'serpentine' pulleys (where the water pump is driven in the opposite rotation by the back of the belt). Check all belts for age, damage and tension. Some early optional equipment such as A/C compressors have a V-belt to themselves. If it's missing, the compressor may seize.

Water pump and fan
All models use a belt-driven water pump and usually a cooling fan driven from the pump hub. Check the pump for leaks, and evidence of drips from the little hole in the snout that indicates a failing seal. They're not expensive, and simple to replace, but make sure you buy the correct replacement – serpentine belts spin the pump 'backwards.' Swapping the engine-driven fan for an electric one is a common and worthwhile modification, if fitted and wired properly.

Radiator
All Foxes, except early four-cylinders, used largely the same height and width radiator. Auto transmission cars have a fluid cooler built into the passenger side of the radiator, and leaks between the coolant and trans fluid sections are rare but not unheard of. Check the fins front and rear for debris damage, and for brown stains caused by overheating. Aluminium aftermarket radiators are common, but cheap eBay units are usually no more efficient than stock, and often worse. Check coolant and heater hoses for perishing, and, if the heater core's been bypassed, be suspicious (see page 56).

A good quality aluminium radiator and twin electric fan setup can help keep your cool, while freeing up extra horsepower ...

Overflow/screen washer bottle

Early models used a large square plastic container on the driver's side inner fender that holds half radiator coolant overflow and half screenwash. Later models hid the screenwash tank under the driver's side fender, with just the filler neck poking into the engine bay, while the coolant overflow was mounted to the radiator fan shroud. Check that the screenwash works, because changing the pump on later models is a pain.

An early screen wash/
coolant overflow tank.

The stock air filter on this early 5.0 draws in cool air from the fenderwell.

Radiator core support

The core support is the box section on which the radiator sits, which looks heavy-duty but isn't. It gets rusty from road salt and spray; gets bashed in by accidents, road debris and clumsy parking nose-in to kerbs; and gets bent out by people thinking it's a good place to attach a tow rope. It's not, so please don't.

Air intake/turbo

Carburetted models had a large, round air cleaner atop the carb; fuel injected models had a remote filter box with ducting to the throttle body. Check that the filter element is clean and free from detritus, and be wary of filter housings full of oil on carburetted cars, signifying engine blow-by. Aftermarket open-element filters look great but won't improve performance if they're just breathing in hot engine bay air. Turbochargers were still new-tech on mass-produced cars when the 2.3 Turbo debuted, so don't expect great things. Early turbochargers were notoriously difficult to keep in tune, generally unreliable, and have subsequently found little popularity. If you want to restore a turbo car that needs a new/rebuilt turbocharger, check prices and availability before committing – you may be shocked.

Battery

Early Foxes have the battery behind the passenger side headlamp; from 1986 it

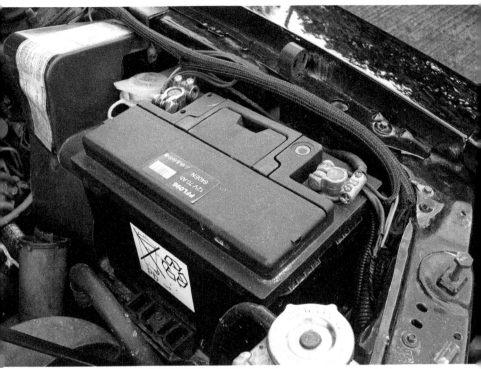

The battery behind the driver's side headlamp. Note the clamp at the base of the battery.

switched to the driver's side. Check the battery for age, condition of the terminals and voltage at rest, plus the condition (and presence!) of the clamp that holds it in place. Batteries can leak acid, and while the tray it sits in is thick plastic, acid and subsequent corrosion will eat the bolts securing the tray, and the chassis rail beneath.

Wiring and ECU

   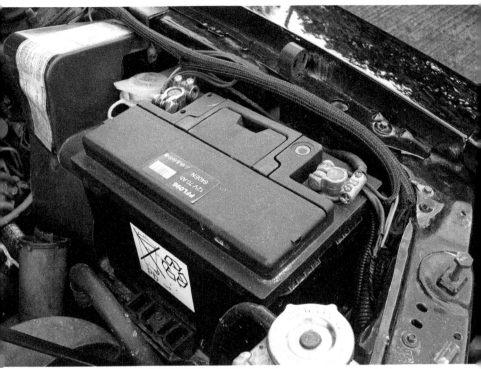

The Electronic Control Unit (ECU) on fuel-injected cars lives behind the passenger side kick panel, and is a pain to get to. They're generally reliable, though; most problems can be traced to engine bay wiring. Check all wiring for burning, chafing, fraying, insulation that's baked hard, bad earths and modification/butchery. Especially check the two main connectors, usually mounted to the back of the EFI intake plenum. One is black, the other white, so they get called the 'salt and pepper shakers' and, if corroded or damaged, mystery faults and 'check engine' lights pop up. EEC-IV is not particularly tunable, so if the seller has made engine mods but kept the stock ECU, expect running problems. The 1988-on OBD-I diagnostic connector lives on the driver's side inner fender, but came before standardised plugs, so you'd need a Ford EEC-specific reader. Or a bent paper clip and a notepad to count the 'check engine' light flashes ...

This aftermarket plug-in ECU lives in the stock location in the passenger side footwell.

The 'salt and pepper' connectors are usually on the back of the plenum, but on Don's car they're next to the throttle body.

The later **AC compressor** is much more compact than the early version.

Air-conditioning

Air-conditioning was a popular option, but all used R12 refrigerant, which is a greenhouse gas and (officially) unavailable. You can upgrade to R134a refrigerant, but you'll have to change several components, which could be time-consuming and expensive. Early (1979-1981) models used cumbersome York or Tecumseh compressors; later models used a more compact unit, though the one on 1983-1988 four-cylinder models proved unreliable. Refrigerant contains a bright dye to highlight leaks so look for luminous stains. For high-performance Fox builders, the A/C is usually the first thing to get junked.

Power steering

Power-assisted steering (PAS) is a popular option – mandatory on all pre-1985 V8s, and standard on all 1985-on models – and I've yet to come across one without it. Check the level and colour of the fluid, and, with the engine running, listen for noisy operation at idle and screeching as you turn toward full lock.

A Fox without power steering is a pretty rare beast.

Brake master and servo/booster   4️⃣ 3️⃣ 2️⃣ 1️⃣

All Foxes had a dual-circuit master cylinder and the vast majority had power brakes with a servo/booster. It was a mandatory option on pre-1986 V8s, and standard thereafter. Check for fluid leaks, especially at the unions on the master cylinder and proportioning valve block below. Boosters on turbo cars suffered from heat-soak, so there should be a heat-reflecting foil on the booster body. If you have any doubts about the brakes, do NOT test drive the car.

Cables   4️⃣ 3️⃣ 2️⃣ 1️⃣

Foxes have cables to the engine for the throttle, auto kickdown and cruise control, plus the clutch and speedometer cables. Check for fraying and adjustment: clutch and speedo cables run close to the exhaust on V6s and V8s, so check they haven't got too close and melted. The condition and adjustment of the throttle valve (TV) cable on overdrive autos is critical, and could ruin the transmission in just a hundred miles if incorrect.

Inner fenders (wings)/chassis rails   4️⃣ 3️⃣ 2️⃣ 1️⃣

Last (under the hood), yet possibly most important, are the inner fenders, firewall and chassis rails. Ford drilled and punched holes in these panels for every conceivable option – it looks like someone on the production line stood in the engine bay and let rip with a shotgun. The most critical spot is the chassis rail box section at the base of the strut turrets. Water and crud get in here, are heated by the nearby exhaust headers on V6 and V8 cars, and the rust runs rampant, out of sight. It's a

This rot in the front rails condemned this Fox. It's a major job to rectify, and can't be ignored.

vital structural area where the subframe attaches, and proper repairs could require engine and subframe removal, so rot in here could be a deal-breaker.

4️⃣ 3️⃣ 2️⃣ 1️⃣
Headlining
Now get inside the car and look up. Convertibles should have nice inner linings on all but the most budget-conscious replacement tops. On tin-top cars, the headliner is usually just thin material glued to fibreboard backing, and, after years of heat and/or damp, the glue fails and the

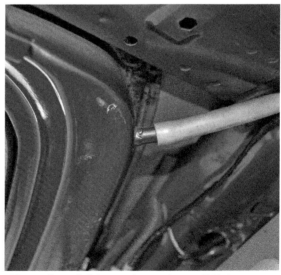

These pipes shrink over time and pop off their spouts. And, yes, I ruined the headlining finding this out ...

material sags. On sunroof cars, the sunroof recess has drain channels with plastic pipes at each corner that drain rainwater down the A- and C-pillars to the rocker panels. Sometimes these pipes get blocked or pop off their spouts, meaning that water drops straight onto the headliner, then into the header rails above the doors, out of sight behind the trims. Cue rust and an in-car sauna. The solution requires headlining removal but, because the vinyl is glued into the sunroof surround and goes brittle with age, the chances of removing the headlining undamaged and reinstalling it neatly are very slim indeed.

Weatherstripping

Check weatherstrip around the door apertures, and between the windows and doorframe, for aging and tears. Replacement is simple, but use the correct weatherstrip; not 'universal' off-the-roll stuff.

Mirrors

Side mirrors can be adjusted manually, remotely via a joystick, or electrically via a switch on the console (1987-on). Check that the adjustment actually works (an MOT fail here in the UK). Interior mirrors are glued to the screen, and the worst they usually suffer is a forest of air fresheners.

Check that electrically-adjustable door mirrors adjust in all directions.

Door trims

Door cards are a trimmed plastic panel on early cars, and upholstered fibreboard on later models. Check for splits and crumbling on plastic ones, and loudspeaker butchery on all. Many have an elasticated door pocket, and when the elastic goes

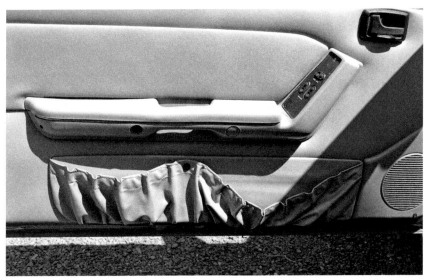

Catching your feet in these slack door pockets gets them looking old really quickly ...

slack you'll catch your foot in it getting in and out, making the problem worse. Replacing the elastic is a pain, but worthwhile. Armrests/door pulls suffer over the years, so check condition and security.

Interior trim panels

The interior plastics – kick panels, rocker trims, A-pillar trims and rear quarter trims – suffer scuffing, scratches and splits from general wear, though most problems arise from being dismantled. They're designed for quick, easy production line assembly, often using little plastic 'fir tree' trim buttons that can't be reused. If they've been dismantled clumsily or refitted with the wrong screws or old fir trees, they'll never fit properly.

Rear seats

Rear seats get less wear than the fronts, but check the upholstery and seatbelts (if fitted). On hatches, check that the folding back latches properly.

The folding rear seats on a hatch give you a large, usable cargo area.

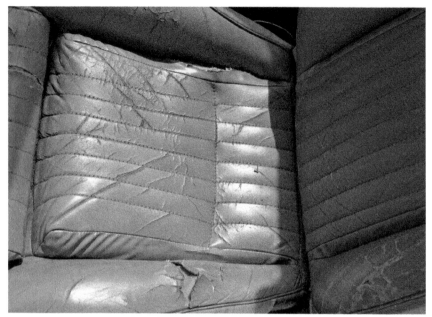

If your car's leather looks like this, you know it's not going to just polish out.

Front seats   ④ ③ ② ①
Foxes came with a long list of interior trim options, and vinyl, cloth or leather upholstery. All suffer over the years; you'll have to judge whether they're beyond saving. Specialists sell replacement upholstery kits, but not in every single variant, and upholstering is a skill that takes patience. Optional Recaro seats (1979-1982) are frighteningly expensive. Check the seats slide on their rails, tilt forwards and latch back securely, and that electric or manual adjustment still works. Check seatbelts for fraying, and smooth extension and rewind.

Centre console   ④ ③ ② ①
Most Foxes came with some sort of console and/or armrest, so check its condition. The armrest is often used by the less limber to help themselves in and out, so may be worn or broken. On later cars, the chances of the ashtray lid NOT being broken are very slim. Check soft gaiters around shifters and parking brake levers.

Sound systems   ④ ③ ② ①
All Foxes had various radios, cassette players and even eight-tracks on the options sheet, but many will have been upgraded over the years. Pre-1985 models used shaft-mount units; later models used DIN standard sized units. You can buy new shaft-mount head units with all modern features, and there are off-the-shelf fitting and wiring kits to adapt modern DIN units into the later dash or console, so there's no excuse for dash/wiring butchery. Premium sound systems used a separate amplifier mounted on the transmission tunnel behind the console, so if you're upgrading the head unit you'll need to bypass the amp.

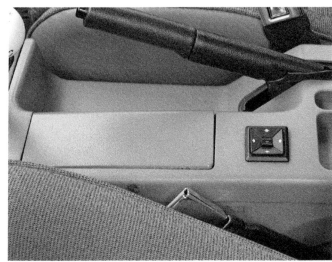

A rare piece indeed – a late-model ashtray that's **NOT** broken!

The original AM/FM radio/cassette in Don's beautiful 1979 Capri.

Heating and air-conditioning

The large box containing the blower fan, heater core, A/C evaporator and ventilation diverters and ducting is mounted to the firewall behind the dash. Heater cores commonly spring leaks with age, but changing them is a dashboard-out job and a huge pain in the ... Check the control levers or rotary controls move smoothly and easily, and that all blower fan speed settings work. If they don't, suspect the resistors and it's PITA time again.

Dashboard

Early models had a square, flat-faced dash with a padded flat top; later models had a more shaped, all-plastic dash. The earlier dash top is more prone to sunbaking and cracking, but also easier to change. However, they're usually colour-matched to the interior/upholstery, limiting your secondhand choice.

Early cars had a more flat-fronted dash ...

Instruments

All Foxes are fairly well instrumented for the period, with all instruments in one cluster, though some had a separate time clock. Speedos are cable driven, so a needle doing the Riverdance as you drive suggests a worn cable. Most pre-1989 models had the Federally-mandated 85mph speedo; some Canadian and export models had a kilometres-per-hour speedo. Watch for warning lights, especially 'check engine' and airbag (1990-on) lights that either stay lit or are suspiciously absent ...

... though the instruments are all in one cluster behind that outer trim.

4️⃣ 3️⃣ 2️⃣ 1️⃣

Switchgear

Check that all dash switches do what they're supposed to, especially the main headlamp switch and the dip/high beam control on the column. The early pull-out headlamp switches fail if overloaded by uprated headlamp bulbs or similar – there's no relay in the system – and the rotary dash illumination dimmer can be temperamental. Switch the lights on and open the door – do you hear a noise? That's the warning buzzer, though most sound like an asthmatic parrot being

Check the switches in the 'wings' on each side of the instruments, and the rather large and clumsy stalk switch on the steering column.

strangled. Many owners remove them, and who can blame them?

Pedals

Check pedals for secure mounting and correlate the pedal pad wear to the odometer reading. One issue is the clutch cable self-adjuster on manual cars from the mid-eighties onward. The clutch pedal operates a shaft that turns the quadrant, a nylon self-adjusting ratchet mechanism to take up slack in the cable, which wears out with use. Many owners replace the nylon quadrant with a solid aluminium one and an adjustable clutch cable, which is fine.

Steering wheel

Foxes have used plenty of different styles of steering wheel, so check all for general condition. The tilt column option ended in 1989, when airbags arrived. Check that the horn button works, and, if the car has cruise control, check that those buttons work (if possible). If they're temperamental, this could be due to the slip-ring or clockspring electrical connections between wheel and column, which are tricky to fix.

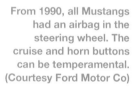

From 1990, all Mustangs had an airbag in the steering wheel. The cruise and horn buttons can be temperamental. (Courtesy Ford Motor Co)

Carpets

The carpet, from halfway up the firewall to the back seat, and from door to door, is one moulded piece. Replacements are available and reasonably priced, and fitting is straightforward but time-consuming as much of the interior needs to be removed. If it's been water damaged, cure the leaks first or the new carpet will go the same way. Consider replacing the damp-retaining sound deadener at the same time.

Trunk

Check the trunk for overall condition of the side panels and the lining or carpet – on hatches, this carpet extends up the rear seat – and check the weatherstripping

This board stops the carpet sagging into the spare wheel well.

all the way around the trunk aperture. Under the carpet/lining is a shaped board covering the spare wheel and jack – check there's not a puddle in there. Foxes used space-saver spares and, as they rarely get used, this could be the one it left the factory with. Would you trust a tyre that old? Some models, mostly convertibles, used a lightweight aluminium space-saver.

④ ③ ② ①
Wheels & tyres
Foxes came with a wide variety of wheels, from early base-model steels

This '79 base model wears very basic wheels and whitebands ... (Courtesy Ford Motor Co)

... while this '79 5.0 coupe has the metric TRX forged alloy wheels.
(Courtesy Ford Motor Co)

Late model GT 'turbines' are great if you like cleaning your wheels with a
toothbrush ...

... but the LX 'ten-hole' wheels are much lower-maintenance.

with bias-ply blackwalls to the 1991-on 16in Pony alloy wheels. Check the condition of the wheels, whether they're appropriate to your car, and the age, condition and speed rating of the tyres. The handsome, forged aluminium wheels in the 1979-1984 TRX handling package were a very odd size. In the late seventies, Michelin decided that it was dumb to have tyres measured in millimetres on wheels measured in inches, so it created radial tyres for metric rim diameters. Ford (USA and Europe), Jaguar, BMW and others jumped on the bandwagon, but it was short-lived and replacement 195/65R390 (1979-1982) and 220/55VR390 (1983-1984) tyres soon became expensive and hard to find. Reproduction 390mm (about 15.3in) tyres are available, but frighteningly expensive, so unless you're looking to win the concours, source other wheels.

Front sway bar [4] [3] [2] [1]
It's time to get underneath the car, so hoist it up ... safely. Check the front anti-roll/sway-bar bushes and brackets, and the end-link bushes where they bolt to the lower arms. End-link bushes wear out, but they're cheap and simple to replace.

These bushes are ruined, but they're cheap enough to replace.

K-member

The K-member is the front subframe that carries the engine, steering and front suspension. I've never known one to rust out, but check for damage, and check the points where it bolts to the bodyshell for corrosion. Check the engine mounts, which can go soft, and the underside of the engine for leaks and oil pan damage.

Steering rack

All Foxes had rack and pinion steering, the majority having standard or optional power-assistance. Check the bushes where the rack bolts to the K-member, which go soft if they get oily. Check for looseness or play in the inner tie-rods, the rod ends at the spindle, and the shaft joints between steering column and rack. Check rubber gaiters on tie-rods and rod-ends for splits. Power steering pipes can perish or rust out, usually at the steering rack end.

This is where the forward K-member mounts join the body – a common rot-spot.

If these pipes rust out, you'll lose all the power-assisted steering fluid very quickly.

Pressing ball joints in and out of the lower arms is a lot of work to save a few bucks.

Lower arms

The lower arms are sturdy pressings, but check the inner bushes for wear, and the pressed-in ball joints for excess play and split rubber boots. You can replace the ball-joint, but replacing the whole arm is much easier.

Front springs

Front springs sit between the lower arm and the K-member with rubber insulators at the top, and varied between the soft-riding base models and the sporting GTs. Changing these springs is a job for

Don't attempt to remove or refit the front springs unless you're properly equipped and experienced.

the competent, confident and thrill-seekers only – any compressed coil spring is a potential bone-breaker/killer.

Front hubs & brakes

All Foxes had front disc brakes with single piston callipers, with hub and rotor cast

in one piece, so check the wheel bearing for free play and noise. All production models used a four-lug, 4.25in/108mm PCD hub; SVOs and '93 Cobras used five-lug, 4.5in/114.3mm hubs. Pre-1982 non-V8 cars used puny 9.3in/263mm rotors; V8s and 1982-1986 models used 10in/254mm rotors; 1987-on V8s used 10.84in/278mm rotors, and even these were only just enough for V8s. Factory and aftermarket upgrades are available and worthwhile, especially on modified V8s.

The factory disc brakes, even on late model V8s, were marginal at best so any upgrades have got to be a bonus.

Front struts

These are MacPherson-style struts (with the spring mounted separately) containing the shock absorber and pivoting on a rubber-bushed mount in the strut tower. Aftermarket adjustable top mounts allow caster and camber adjustment but need setting up at a good alignment shop; not a shade-tree mechanic's best guess.

These adjustable top mounts are only worthwhile if you're going to have the alignment properly set up.

④ ③ ② ①
Forward chassis rails

Following on from page 51, those structurally critical rails run half the length of the car, from the bumper, down under the toeboards and alongside the transmission. Check them, and the triangular torque boxes under the toeboards for evidence of rust, crash damage and careless jacking.

Transmission ④ ③ ② ①

Fox automatic transmissions included the three-speed C3 behind early 2.3s, the C4 on most early-eighties cars, the C5 (a C4 with lock-up convertor) on 1982 models, and the A4LD four-speed on later four-cylinders. Most common is the 1984-on AOD (automatic overdrive) four-speed. The C3 and A4LD are fine behind stock four-pots. The C4 is much loved and can be built to take plenty of power, but the C5 is best avoided. The AOD is a good unit with a long-legged overdrive, but watch for worn bands and slipping in top gear – the overdrive reduces freeway revs so much that the

The rails and torque boxes on this freshly-media-blasted shell are (fortunately) excellent.

pump can't maintain enough pressure to keep the overdrive band firmly engaged, and they can't be adjusted like those on C-series transmissions. A shift kit will help, but rebuilt AODs aren't cheap. Check the oil pan and tailshaft seal for leaks and damage, and the TV cable or vacuum modulator pipes for damage.

Early manuals used Ford's SROD (single-rail overdrive) or T-04 four-speed, which are okay behind stock motors, but not great otherwise. From 1981, Ford began using the well-loved T-5 four-speed plus overdrive fifth. From 1985, Ford upgraded to the T-5 World Class, which is smoother but no stronger; 1990-1993 V8s used the pick of the bunch with a tougher first gear set. Performance enthusiasts love the five-speed, but even a stock 5.0 EFI was pushing the T-5's torque handling capabilities; hotter engines and/or drag strip use will soon kill it. If the little metal tag is still attached by one of the tailshaft housing bolts, the number that begins 1352- can be decoded online to learn more.

Driveshaft ④ ③ ② ①

All Foxes used a one-piece driveshaft, and they're largely interchangeable. Early models used a 2.75in/70mm shaft; from 1983 on it was 3in/76mm in diameter. Check the universal joints at each end for wear and, if the UJ has a grease fitting, whether it has been greased recently.

Rocker panels ④ ③ ② ①

The rockers, or sills, are another structurally important and rust-prone area. They get salt and road debris thrown at the outside, the sunroof drains empty into the inside, then along comes a lazy mechanic with a floor-jack ... Check for rust, damage, and clear drain slots. Plastic GT skirts can hide a lot.

Floorpans

Check every inch of the floors for evidence of rust, crash damage and that fool with the floor-jack, especially around the front seats' rear mounting bolts where heavyweight drivers throwing themselves in and out of the car caused the metal to split; 1985-on models

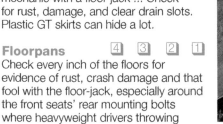

Those plastic skirts can hide many sins.

had reinforcing plates but check anyway. Between the end of the forward chassis rails and the crossmember that mounts the rear suspension arms, there's not a lot of structural strength. Aftermarket subframe connectors tie the two together, and they're a good idea whether you're chasing performance or not – they really tighten the car up. Weld-on connectors are preferable to bolt-ons, and convertibles will need a little extra ingenuity.

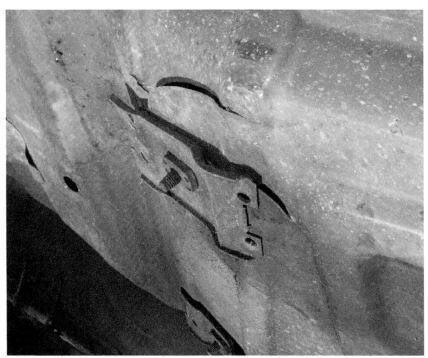

This otherwise perfect floor has split around the seat mounting bolts.

Weld-on subframe connectors tighten the shell beautifully, and are strong enough to jack up on.

Rear suspension arms & springs

☐4 ☐3 ☐2 ☐1

Rear suspension arms are pressed steel U-section; the lower arms are straight fore-and-aft and carry the coil springs, while the upper ones are triangulated for lateral location. Each has a rubber bush in each end, and worn bushes can cause very strange handling; the worst culprit being the upper arm's forward end. Coil spring rules are the same as on page 63, but rear springs have rubber isolators top and bottom. Rear sway bars are solid-mounted to the lower arms, and 1982-1984 V8s had add-on traction bars to prevent wind-up.

This suspension bush isn't just worn, it's trying to escape!

Rear shocks

☐4 ☐3 ☐2 ☐1

Check all brackets and bushes, and the shock itself for leaks. Lower shock brackets are much sturdier on later models. From mid-1984, Ford fitted an extra pair of shocks to hotter models, running horizontally from the top of the axle tubes to the chassis rails behind. Called 'Quad-Shocks,' they prevent wheel hop under hard acceleration.

Rear end/axle

☐4 ☐3 ☐2 ☐1

Foxes used three rear axle variants: the early 6.75in/171mm, the 7.5in/190mm,

If your Fox has any of this behaviour in its future, you should definitely have the 8.8in axle ... (Courtesy Martin Drake)

and the 1986-on 8.8in/225mm, and all are interchangeable. The feeble 6.75 is okay for a four- or six-cylinder cruiser, the 7.5 is likewise fine behind a stock motor, but the tough 8.8 is the performance choice. A little in-and-out movement in the wheel bearing is acceptable but bearing play could mean a damaged axle shaft. Check the differential rear cover for damage – if the clown with the floor-jack has bent the cover, the oil leaks out. Traction-Lok locker differentials were optional from 1981 and standard on 1983-on V8s. It's worth having, but uses a special oil additive, and friction plates that wear out with miles and/or abuse are tricky to replace.

④ ③ ② ①
Rear brakes
All Foxes bar the SVO and 1993 Cobra used rear drum brakes. Most used a 9in/228mm drum with 1.75in/44mm wide shoes; pre-1983 models could be optioned with

Only the SVO/SVT Foxes had discs on the rear, but upgrades are quite easy. Adam's LX still has drums.

10in/254mm by 2in/51mm heavy-duty drums. Check for fluid leaks, dragging/stuck shoes and grinding noises, and if you have any doubts about the brakes, don't test-drive the car!

Fuel tank

The fuel tank is suspended beneath the trunk floor on two steel straps, which rust. Early models had a shallow tank with the sender in the front; later EFI cars had a deeper tank to provide increased range and room for the in-tank pump, with the sender on top. The steel tank often sits inside a protective plastic shield. On EFI cars, check the fuel filter – has it been changed this millennium, with the correct clips holding the push-on pipes? CFI cars had a low-pressure in-tank pump feeding a high-pressure external pump. Check the rubber sealing ring where the filler neck enters the tank.

Trunk floor

Check every inch of the trunk floor and wheel wells for rust and damage, especially the chassis rails and the drop-offs where the trunk floor drops down to join the rear quarters behind the wheels.

The most common rot spots are on each side, behind the rear wheels. This floor was, amazingly, like new.

Brake & fuel pipes

Foxes used steel brake and fuel pipes, and failure could prove lethal, so check every inch for rust, damage and secure mounting, and all flexible pipes for chafing, perishing and ethanol damage. The main front-to-rear brake pipe crosses the chassis rail just ahead of the passenger-side rear wheel, covered by a bolt-on plate to prevent crushing. This plate is a crap-trap, and the pipe can rust through here undetected. Also check the parking brake cables – if lazy auto drivers just park with the transmission in 'P' without using the parking brake, the cables seize; also, the parking brake operates the drums' self-adjusting mechanism.

Exhaust

All Foxes left the factory with at least one catalytic converter; some had four. Many get removed in pursuit of horsepower, but will the car still pass emissions tests or roadside 'sniffer' checks in your area? The aftermarket is full of Fox performance exhausts, but while V8s sound great on straight-through mufflers, your neighbours/ local cops may disagree and, on longer trips, the boom and drone may prove tiring. The bigger the exhaust diameter, the less ground clearance you'll have, and the tighter things will be around the rear axle; lowering springs exacerbate the problem, and many will have D-shaped pipes ...

Lowered springs and fat exhausts equal D-shaped pipes and scraping over every bump in the road.

Evaluation calculation
Add up all the points
304 = excellent, possibly concours
228 = very good
152 = average
76 = poor
Cars scoring over 212 should be completely usable, with little major work required. Cars scoring 152-211 points may be drivable, but will require careful assessment. Cars scoring below 152 points are likely to need serious remedial surgery or full restoration.

10 Auctions
– sold! Another way to buy your dream

Auction pros & cons
Pros: Assuming that this is a local car auction and not a major collector car auction, prices will usually be lower than those of dealers or private sellers and you might grab a real bargain on the day. Auctioneers have usually established clear title with the seller, and you can often examine documentation relating to the vehicle at the venue.

Cons: You have to rely on a sketchy catalogue description of condition and history. The opportunity to inspect is limited and you cannot drive the car. Auction cars are often a little below par and may require some work. It's easy to overbid. There will usually be a buyer's premium to pay in addition to the auction hammer price.

Which auction?
Auctions by established auctioneers are advertised in car magazines and on the auction houses' websites. A catalogue, or a simple printed list of the lots, might only be available a day or two ahead of the sale, though lots are often listed and pictured on auctioneers' websites much earlier. Contact the auction company to ask if previous auction selling prices are available as this is useful information – details of past sales are often available on websites.

Catalogue, entry fee and payment details
When you purchase the catalogue of the vehicles in the auction, it often acts as a ticket allowing two people to attend the viewing days and the auction. Catalogue details tend to be comparatively brief, but will include information such as 'one owner from new, low mileage, full service history,' etc. It will also usually show a guide price to give you some idea of what to expect to pay, and will tell you what is charged as a 'Buyer's premium'. The catalogue will also contain details of acceptable forms of payment. At the fall of the hammer, an immediate deposit is usually required, the balance payable within 24 hours. If the plan is to pay cash, there may be a cash limit. Some houses will accept payment by debit card; sometimes they'll accept credit or charge cards, but these often incur an extra charge. A bank draft or bank transfer may have to be arranged in advance with your own bank as well as with the auction house. No car will be released before ALL payments are cleared. If delays occur in payment transfers, then storage charges can accrue.

Buyer's premium
A buyer's premium will be added to the hammer price: don't overlook this in your calculations. It's not unusual for there to be a further state tax or local tax on the purchase price and/or on the buyer's premium.

Viewing
In some instances, it's possible to view on the day, or days before, as well as in the hours prior to the auction. There are auction officials available who are willing to help out by opening engine and luggage compartments, and to allow you to inspect the interior. While they may start the engine for you, a test drive is out of the question.

Crawling under and around the car as much as you want is permitted, but you can't suggest that the car you are interested in be jacked up, or attempt to do the job yourself. You can also ask to see any documentation available.

Bidding

Before you take part in the auction, decide your maximum bid… and stick to it! It may take a while for the auctioneer to reach the lot you're interested in, so use that time to observe how other bidders behave. When it's the turn of your car, attract the auctioneer's attention and make an early bid. The auctioneer will then look to you for a reaction every time another bid is made. Usually, the bids will be in fixed increments until the bidding slows, when smaller increments will often be accepted before the hammer falls. If you want to withdraw from the bidding, make sure the auctioneer understands your intentions – a clear shake of the head when he or she looks to you for the next bid should do the trick!

Assuming that you are the successful bidder, the auctioneer will note your card or paddle number, and from that moment on you will be responsible for the vehicle.

If the car is unsold, either because it failed to reach the reserve or because there was little interest, it may be possible to negotiate with the owner, via the auctioneers, after the sale is over.

Successful bid

There are two more matters to think about: how to get the car home, and insurance. If you can't drive the car, your own or a hired trailer is one way; another is to have the vehicle shipped using a local company. The auction house will have details of such companies.

Insurance for immediate cover can usually be purchased on-site or online, but it may be more cost-effective to make arrangements with your own insurance company in advance, then call to confirm the full details.

eBay and other online auctions

Online auctions could land you a car at a bargain price, though you'd be foolish to bid without examining the car first, something most vendors encourage. A useful feature of eBay and others is that the geographical location of the car is shown, so you can narrow your choices to those within a realistic radius of home. Be prepared to be 'sniped' – outbid in the final moments of the auction. Remember, your bid is binding, and it can be very, very difficult to get restitution in the case of a crooked vendor fleecing you – caveat emptor! There are plenty of scams out there, so don't part with any cash without being sure that the vehicle does actually exist, is as described, and is the vendor's property to sell.

Auctioneers

Bonhams www.bonhams.com
British Car Auctions www.bca.com
Christies www.christies.com
Coys www.coys.co.uk

eBay www.eBay.com or www.eBay.co.uk
H&H www.handh.co.uk
Shannons www.shannons.com.au
Silver www.silverauctions.com

11 Paperwork
– correct documentation is essential!

The paper trail

Classic, collector and prestige cars usually come with a large portfolio of paperwork accumulated and passed on by a succession of proud owners. This documentation represents the real history of the car and from it can be deduced the level of care the car has received, how much it's been used, which specialists have worked on it and the dates of major repairs and restorations. All of this information will be priceless to you as the new owner, so be very wary of cars with little paperwork to support their claimed history.

Registration documents

All countries/states have some form of registration for private vehicles whether it's like the American 'pink slip' system or the British 'log book' system.

It is essential to check that the registration document is genuine, that it relates to the car in question, and that all the vehicle's details are correctly recorded, including chassis/VIN and engine numbers (if these are shown). If you are buying from the previous owner, his or her name and address will be recorded in the document: this will not be the case if you are buying from a dealer.

In the UK the current (Euro-aligned) registration document is named 'V5C,' and is printed in coloured sections of blue, green and pink. The blue section relates to the car specification, the green section has details of the new owner and the pink section is sent to the DVLA in the UK when the car is sold. A small section in yellow deals with selling the car within the motor trade.

Previous ownership records

Due to the introduction of important new legislation on data protection, it is no longer possible to acquire, from the British DVLA, a list of previous owners of a car you own, or are intending to purchase. This scenario will also apply to dealerships and other specialists, from who you may wish to make contact and acquire information on previous ownership and work carried out.

If the car has a foreign registration, there may be expensive and time-consuming formalities to complete. Do you really want the hassle?

Roadworthiness certificate

Most country/state administrations require that vehicles are regularly tested to prove that they are safe to use on the public highway and do not produce excessive emissions. In the UK that test (the 'MOT') is carried out at approved testing stations, for a fee. In the USA the requirement varies, but most states insist on an emissions test every two years as a minimum, while the police are charged with pulling over unsafe-looking vehicles.

In the UK the test is required on an annual basis once a vehicle becomes three years old. Of particular relevance for older cars is that the certificate issued includes the mileage reading recorded at the test date and, therefore, becomes an independent record of that car's history. Ask the seller if previous certificates are available. Without an MOT the vehicle should be trailered to its new home, unless you insist that a valid MOT is part of the deal. (Not such a bad idea this, as at least you will know the car was roadworthy on the day it was tested and you don't need to wait for the old certificate to expire before having the test done.) In the UK, vehicles over 40 years old on May 20th each year, are exempt from MOT testing. Owners can still have the test carried out if they so wish.

Road licence
The administration of every country/state charges some kind of tax for the use of its road system, the actual form of the 'road licence' and, how it is displayed, varying enormously country to country and state to state.

Whatever the form of the 'road licence' it must relate to the vehicle carrying it, and must be present and valid if the car is to be driven on the public highway legally.

Changed legislation in the UK means that the seller of a car must surrender any existing road fund licence, and it is the responsibility of the new owner to re-tax the vehicle at the time of purchase and before the car can be driven on the road. It's therefore vital to see the Vehicle Registration Certificate (V5C) at the time of purchase, and to have access to the New Keeper Supplement (V5C/2), allowing the buyer to obtain road tax immediately.

In the UK, classic vehicles 40 years old or more, on the 1st January each year get free road tax. It is still necessary to renew the tax status every year, even if there is no change.

If the car is untaxed because it has not been used for a period of time, the owner has to inform the licensing authorities.

Certificates of authenticity
For many makes of collectible car it is possible to get a certificate proving the age and authenticity (eg engine and chassis numbers, paint colour and trim) of a particular vehicle, these are sometimes called 'Heritage Certificates' and if the car comes with one of these it is a definite bonus. If you want to obtain one, the relevant owners club is the best starting point.

If the car has been used in European classic car rallies it may have a FIVA (Fédération International des Véhicules Anciens) certificate. The so-called 'FIVA Passport,' or 'FIVA Vehicle Identity Card,' enables organisers and participants to recognise whether or not a particular vehicle is suitable for individual events. If you want to obtain such a certificate go to www.fbhvc.co.uk or www.fiva.org. There will be similar organisations in other countries too.

Valuation certificate
Hopefully, the vendor will have a recent valuation certificate, or letter signed by a recognised expert stating how much he, or she, believes the particular car to be worth (such documents, together with photos, are usually needed to get 'agreed value' insurance). Generally such documents should act only as confirmation of your own assessment of the car rather than a guarantee of value as the expert has probably not seen the car in the flesh. The easiest way to find out how to obtain a formal valuation is to contact the owners club.

Service history
Often these cars will have been serviced at home by enthusiastic (and hopefully capable) owners for a good number of years. Nevertheless, try to obtain as much service history and other paperwork pertaining to the car as you can. Naturally,

dealer stamps, or specialist garage receipts score most points in the value stakes. However, anything helps in the great authenticity game, items like the original bill of sale, handbook, parts invoices and repair bills, adding to the story and the character of the car. Even a brochure correct to the year of the car's manufacture is a useful document and something that you could well have to search hard to locate in future years. If the seller claims that the car has been restored, then expect receipts and other evidence from a specialist restorer.

If the seller claims to have carried out regular servicing, ask what work was completed, when, and seek some evidence of it being carried out. Your assessment of the car's overall condition should tell you whether the seller's claims are genuine.

Restoration photographs
If the seller tells you that the car has been restored, then expect to be shown a series of photographs taken while the restoration was under way. Pictures taken at various stages, and from various angles, should help you gauge the thoroughness of the work. If you buy the car, ask if you can have all the photographs as they form an important part of the vehicle's history. It's surprising how many sellers are happy to part with their car and accept your cash, but want to hang on to their photographs! In the latter event, you may be able to persuade the vendor to get a set of copies made.

12 What's it worth?

– let your head rule your heart

Condition

If the car you've been looking at is really bad, then you've probably not bothered to use the marking system in chapter 9. You may not have even got as far as using that chapter at all! If you did use chapter 9, you'll know whether the car is in Excellent/Concours, Good, Average or Poor condition or, perhaps, somewhere in between these categories.

Many classic/collector car magazines run a regular price guide. If you haven't bought the latest editions, do so now and compare their suggested values for the model you're thinking of buying; also, look at the auction prices they're reporting. Values are increasing, but some models will always be more sought after than others. Trends can change, too. The values published in these magazines tend to vary from one magazine to another, as do their scales of condition, so read carefully the guidance notes they provide. Bear in mind that a car that is truly a recent show winner could be worth more than the highest scale published. Assuming that the car you have in mind is not in show/concours condition, then relate the level of condition that you judge the car to be in with the appropriate guide price. How does the figure compare with the asking price? Before you begin haggling with the seller, consider how any variation from standard specification might affect the car's value. If you are buying from a dealer, remember that there will be a dealer's premium on the price.

Desirable options/extras

Foxes have been through various trim levels, each with dozens of options. Early examples had the base model, the luxury Ghia or the sporty Cobra. From 1982 this became the L, the GL, the GLX or sporting GT, and from 1986 onward just the LX or GT.

The early Cobra was mostly just an appearance package. This is a 1979 model.
(Courtesy Ford Motor Co)

This is Kevin See's beautifully restored '79 Pace Car. (Courtesy Kevin See)

Discounting the Foxes modified by third parties such as Roush, Saleen and McLaren, there have been many factory special editions. Straight away there was the 1979 Indy Pace Car replica with special trim and graphics, but Ford made over 10,000 of these, so calling them a limited edition is a stretch. Find a good original one, though, and it's a guaranteed collectible.

The 1983 GT Turbo with the four-pot engine is a rarity, with only 556 made. In mid-1984 came the 20th Anniversary edition: over 5000 hatches and convertibles, all painted Oxford White with special trim, mostly V8s but a few hundred Turbo fours. If you find one, keep it original.

Ford's new Special Vehicle Operations department created the SVO Mustang in 1984, a tweaked turbo four-pot built for poise and handling. With between 175 and 205hp, they really got the turbo recipe right, but they were expensive, and buyers preferred the V8 grunt. Around 10,000 were sold between 1984 and 1986, and collectors prize them.

Between April 1989 and June 1990, all Mustangs were badged "25th Anniversary" – they were not a special edition!

In 1990, Ford built over 4000 Special Edition LX convertibles in new Emerald Green, including 30 for a special 7Up promotion that never happened – they're worth preserving.

Ford saved the best until last with the 1993 Cobra. Designed by the SVO team (now named SVT), they had all the best bits and a 235hp V8. Around 5000

This 1986 SVO would be one of the last with the flush-fitting headlamps.
(Courtesy Ford Motor Co)

All Mustangs in a
more than 12 month
production period
wore this badge.

The 1993 SVT Cobra was a superb swansong for the Fox. (Courtesy Ford Motor Co)

were built, including 107 Cobra R race-only models, and they're already pricey collectibles.

From 1982 onwards, Ford made SSP (Special Service Performance) Mustangs, mostly coupes, for police highway patrol and government work. They were well built and well looked after, but worked hard.

Undesirable features

Mostly, this will boil down to personal taste. Some love the pre-1987 four-headlight cars – one of the best Mustang forums online is foureyedpride.com – while many

You might prefer the four-headlamp look, such as this 1981 Mercury Capri Black Magic special edition ... (Courtesy Ford Motor Co)

... or you may prefer to be ice, ice cool in this '87 'Aero front' convertible.
(Courtesy Ford Motor Co)

prefer the 1987-on Aero-look. Performance builders look for coupes and hatches, while cruisers may prefer convertibles. Do you want the super-seventies style of a red interior and vinyl roof, the eighties Vanilla Ice-cool of a white GT convertible, or a Chuck Seitsinger-style Street Outlaw tarmac terrorist?

Engine-wise, the early 2.3 Turbo has few fans, and the 1980-1982 255-cube V8 is fine for cruising to car shows, but anyone seeking performance should start with a 302. Early two-barrel carb V8s make the right noises but are underwhelming; 1983-on four-barrels and 1986-on EFI models with roller cams and stainless tube headers are the performers.

There were almost three million Foxes built, and rarely will any two be exactly identical, so only you can judge what 'undesirable features' are. If you're looking for performance or a good investment, always choose a V8.

Striking a deal

Negotiate on the basis of your condition assessment, mileage and fault rectification costs. Also take into account the car's specification. Be realistic about the value, but don't be completely intractable: a small compromise on the part of the vendor and/ or buyer will often facilitate a deal at little real cost.

13 Do you really want to restore?

– it'll take longer and cost more than you think

Beginners may not be aware of these restoration home truths. First, estimate how much time and money the job will take to complete. Now quadruple those figures and you might be closer to the truth.

Second, you know those TV shows where they buy a classic car, do a few restoration jobs and then flip it for a profit? How often do you think that happens in real life? 'Reality TV' is still TV; not reality.

Right now, I'd say that unless you've picked up a peach of a Fox at bargain-bin money, you're unlikely to make a profit, so you should be building it for yourself. Buying a ⬤x5000 Fox and spending ⬤x10,000 on it does not automatically make it worth ⬤x15,000; however, if you get ⬤x15,000-worth of smiles out of it, it was money well spent.

From the outset, be honest with yourself. If you work nine-to-five, then work on the car in the evenings so you can enjoy it at weekends, that's great. If you work away, or have little spare time due to family and other commitments, how much time can you really give the car?

Do you have the space? A Fox takes up about 86ft^2/8m^2, but strip it down and you'll need four times that; pile stuff up, and things get lost and damaged. Do you have indoor working space? You can build a Fox outdoors, sure, but trying to weld or paint in between rain showers will sap your enthusiasm. Being at the mercy of the weather is a real sinkhole for motivation.

A full strip down rotisserie restoration is extremely time-consuming and expensive, but you will get great results ...

... or you could just leave it looking shabby and enjoy the hell out of it.

Do you have the money? Of course, you can build a Fox on a tight budget, but nothing is free. The little, insignificant things – grinding discs, nuts 'n' bolts, welding wire, electrical terminals, sandpaper, hose clips, etc – soon add up. Always factor delivery into prices. Most Mustang specialist and performance suppliers are in the USA so, outside North America, shipping, import duties and taxes can easily double an item's cost. Are you paying a mechanic or bodyshop to do the work? If so, remember that their estimate of hours and costs is just that: an estimate, based on a quick look around the car. You can bet they'll find more that needs doing once they start digging.

All of this may sound really negative, but if you're not truthful with yourself you'll have a miserable experience, and may end up with a part-finished Fox rotting under a tarp on your driveway, mumbling "Not for sale ... gonna fix it up someday." Don't fall into that trap! Be honest!

Whether you're looking for a quick fixer-upper or a ground-up rotisserie restoration, make a plan, have a good idea what you want from the finished car, and go for it. Don't be afraid to seek advice from your new online Fox friends – getting advice from real car guys/girls is easy; it's getting them to shut up that's hard. There's a whole world of knowledge online, but also a whole world of BS, so choose carefully. At the end, you should have the Fox that YOU want; not what someone else thinks it should be, or what fashion dictates. It's YOUR Fox, be proud of it.

14 Paint problems
– bad complexion, including dimples, pimples and bubbles

Paint faults generally occur due to lack of protection/ maintenance or to poor preparation prior to a respray or touch-up. Some of the following conditions may be present in the car you're looking at.

Orange peel
This appears as an uneven paint surface, similar to the appearance of the skin of an orange. The fault is caused by the failure of the atomised paint droplets to flow into each other when they hit the surface. It's sometimes possible to rub out the effect with proprietary paint cutting/ rubbing compound or very fine grades of abrasive paper, but a respray may be necessary in severe cases. Consult a bodyshop or paint shop for advice on your particular car.

Cracking
Severe cases are likely to have been caused by too heavy an application of paint, or filler beneath the paint. Also, insufficient stirring of the paint before application can lead to the components being improperly mixed, and cracking can result. Incompatibility with the paint already on the panel can have a similar effect. To rectify the problem, it is necessary to rub down to a smooth, sound finish before respraying the problem area.

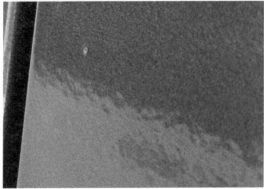

Orange peel.

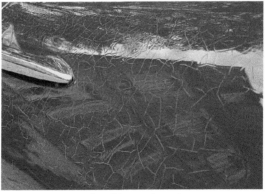

Cracking and crazing.

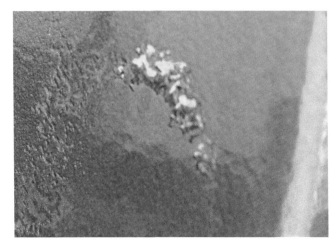

Paint reaction.

Crazing

Sometimes the paint takes on a crazed rather than a cracked appearance when the problems mentioned under 'Cracking' are present. This problem can also be caused by a reaction between the underlying surface and the new paint. Paint removal and respraying the problem area is usually the only solution.

Blistering

Almost always caused by corrosion of the metal beneath the paint. Usually perforation will be found in the metal, and the damage will almost certainly be worse than that suggested by the area of blistering. The metal will have to be repaired before repainting.

Micro-blistering

Usually the result of an economy respray where inadequate heating has allowed moisture to settle on the car before spraying. Consult a paint specialist, but usually damaged paint will have to be removed before partial or full respraying. Can also be caused by car covers that don't 'breathe'.

Fading

Some colours, especially reds, are prone to fading if subjected to strong sunlight for long periods without the benefit of polish protection. Sometimes proprietary paint restorers and/or paint cutting/rubbing compounds will revive the situation, but often a respray is the only real solution.

Peeling

Often a problem with metallic paintwork when the sealing lacquer becomes damaged and begins to peel off. Poorly applied paint may also peel. The remedy is to strip and start again!

Dimples

Dimples in the paint are caused by polish residue (particularly silicone types) not

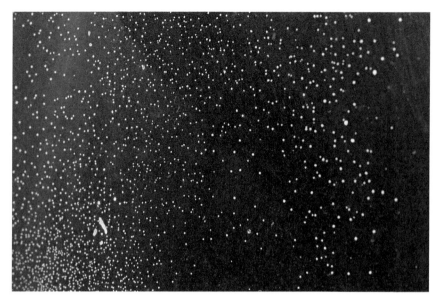
Micro-blistering.

being removed properly before respraying. Paint removal and respraying is the only solution.

Dents
Small dents are often easily cured by the 'Dentmaster' or equivalent process, which sucks or pushes out the dent (as long as the paint surface is still intact). Companies offering dent removal services usually come to your home; Google your local franchise.

15 Problems due to lack of use
– just like their owners, Foxes need exercise!

Cars, like humans, are at their most efficient if they exercise regularly. A run of at least ten miles (16km) once a week is recommended for classics.

Seized components

• Pistons in brake callipers, master and slave cylinders can seize.
• The clutch may seize if the plate becomes stuck to the flywheel due to corrosion.
• Parking brakes can seize if the cables and linkages rust.
• Brake pads and shoes can stick to discs/drums.
• Pistons can seize in their bores due to corrosion.

Okay, clearly this car has been sitting here for a while.

Fluids
• Old, acidic oil can corrode bearings.
• Plain water instead of coolant with corrosion inhibitors can corrode internal waterways. Lack of antifreeze can cause core plugs to be pushed out or even crack the block or head. Silt settling and solidifying can cause overheating.

These brakes haven't seen use for a long time, so don't expect them to work ...

• Brake fluid absorbs moisture from the atmosphere and should be renewed every two years. Old fluid with a high water content can cause corrosion and pistons to seize in callipers/slaves, and can cause brake failure when the water vaporises near hot braking components.

• Gasoline/petrol has a short shelf life, especially modern unleaded with ethanol. Ethanol corrodes non-ferrous metals and rubber components, and is hydroscopic, meaning it absorbs atmospheric moisture and accelerates rusting.

Tyre problems
Tyres that have had the weight of the car on them in a single position for some time will develop flat spots, resulting in some (usually temporary) vibration. The tyre walls

Tyres have a shelf life, and old rubber degrades, so don't trust tyres like this.

may have cracks, blisters or bulges, meaning new tyres are needed. Don't trust old tyres.

Rubber and plastic
Radiator hoses may have perished and split, possibly resulting in the loss of all coolant. Weatherstrips can harden and leak, wiper blades will harden, gaiters/boots can crack, and suspension bushes will perish and disintegrate.

Electrics
The battery will be of little use if it hasn't been charged for many months. Earthing/grounding problems are common when the connectors have corroded. Old bullet and spade type connectors commonly corrode, and will need disconnecting, cleaning and protecting with Vaseline or similar. Wiring insulation will harden and become brittle, and rodents just love chewing on it ...

Exhaust system
Exhaust systems attract condensation, and the exhaust gas makes it acidic, so they corrode very quickly from the inside out.

16 The Community
– key people, organisations and companies in the Mustang world

Until recent years, the Mustang has been predominantly a North American-only model; however, they have been privately exported everywhere, and have legions of enthusiastic owners and fans around the world. Wherever you are, chances are high that there's at least one national owners' club, online fan forum and/or Facebook group.

Although many clubs and specialist restorers/parts suppliers are more likely to concentrate on the sixties classics or late models, Fox ownership is becoming less of a 'fringe' scene and more mainstream, so few are likely to turn you away. Wherever you are in the world, a minute on Google and you're likely to find a club in your country, possibly a group in your area or even a meet in your town.

Right here in Great Britain there's a thriving Mustang Owners' Club (www.mocgb.net), a bustling Facebook community (SimplyMustangsUK) and a Fox-only page (FoxDoctorsUK). The latter has proven invaluable in terms of information, advice, spares and support, and without help from Don Hardy, Stephen Bugg and other UK Fox Doctors, building a Fox would have been twice the work and half the fun. Plus, they all helped a great deal with this book.

Until recently there were many monthly glossy magazines aimed at Mustang fans: *Mustang Monthly*, *Muscle Mustangs* & *Fast Fords*, *Modified Mustangs* & *Fords*, *5.0 Mustangs* & *Super Fords*, *Ford Muscle* and so on. Sadly, many have now disappeared from the news-stands and moved online-only. Foxes still crop up occasionally in the niche titles – here in the UK we have *Street Machine* (www.street-machine.co.uk) or *Classic American* (www.classic-american.com) and Ford-only titles such as *Fast Ford*, *Classic Ford*, *Retro Ford* etc.

Restoration parts suppliers
National Parts Depot – www.npdlink.com
Fox Mustang Restoration – www.foxresto.com
Late Model Restoration – www.lmr.com
CJ Pony Parts – www.cjponyparts.com
American Muscle – www.americanmuscle.com

Performance parts suppliers
All of the above, plus:
Summit Racing Equipment – www.summitracing.com
Jegs – www.jegs.com
Ford Performance – performance.ford.com/parts
Maximum Motorsports – www.maximummotorsports.com
UMI Performance – www.umiperformance.com
BMR Suspension – www.bmrsuspension.com
BBK Performance Parts – www.bbkperformance.com

17 Vital statistics
– essential data at your fingertips

Dimensions
Overall length – max 179.6in
Wheelbase – 100.5in
Overall height – max 52.1in
Overall width – max 69.1in

Build numbers
In all my research, while most sources agree on the total annual build numbers, no two sources seem to completely agree on the breakdown of models, so don't take these figures as gospel!
Mustang – 2,608,812
Capri – 370,689
Total – 2,979,501

Ford Mustang
1979
Coupe base – 156,666
Hatch base – 92,478
Coupe Ghia – 56,351
Coupe Pace Car – 10,478
Hatch Ghia – 36,384
Hatch Cobra – 17,579
Total – 369,936

1980
Coupe base – 128,893
Coupe Ghia – 23,647
Hatch base (inc Cobra) – 98,497
Hatch Ghia – 20,285
Total – 271,322

1981
Coupe base – 77,458
Hatch base (inc Cobra) – 77,399
Coupe Ghia – 13,422
Hatch Ghia – 14,273
Total – 182,552

1982
Coupe base L/GL – 45,316
Hatch GL – 44,549

Coupe GLX – 5828
Hatch GLX – 9926
Hatch GT – 24,799
Total – 130,418

1983
Coupe – 33,201
Hatch LX – 37,586
Convertible GLX – 22,437
Hatch GT – 26,648
Convertible GT – 1001
Total – 120,873

1984
Coupe – 37,680
Hatch LX – 57,542
Hatch GT – 24,150
Convertible LX – 11,344
Convertible GT – 6256
Hatch SVO – 4508
Total – 141,480

1985
Coupe – 56,781
Hatch LX – 46,229
Hatch GT – 36,879
Convertible LX – 9561
Convertible GT – 5549
Hatch SVO – 1515
Total – 156,514

1986
Coupe – 83,774
Hatch LX – 73,633
Hatch GT – 40,678
Convertible LX – 13,058
Convertible GT – 9888
Hatch SVO – 3379
Total – 224,410

1987
Coupe LX – 43,257
Hatch LX – 57,353
Hatch GT – 37,088
Convertible LX – 21,623
Convertible GT – 10,451
Total – 169,772

1988
Coupe LX – 53,221
Hatch LX – 75,636
Hatch GT – 50,294
Convertible LX – 13,900
Convertible GT – 18,174
Total – 211,225

1989
Coupe – 50,560
Hatch – 116,965
Convertible – 42,244
Total – 209,769

1990
Coupe – 22,503
Hatch – 78,728
Convertible – 26,958
Total – 128,189

1991
Coupe – 19,447
Hatch – 57,777
Convertible – 21,513
Total – 98,737

1992
Coupe – 15,717
Hatch – 40,093
Convertible – 23,470
Total – 79,280

1993
Coupe – 24,851
Hatch – 56,977
Convertible – 27,300
Hatch SVT Cobra – 4993
Hatch SVT Cobra R –
  107
Total – 114,335

Mercury Capri (all were hatchbacks)
1979
Base – 68,252
Ghia – 17,712

RS – 14,667
Turbo RS – 9503
Total – 110,144

1980
Base – 64,791
Ghia – 7975
RS – 2080
Turbo RS – 5138
Total – 79,984

1981
Base – 42,463
GS – 7160
RS – 4718
Turbo RS – 17
Black Magic – 4013
White Magic – 575
Total – 58,946

1982
Base – 20,981
L – 1079
GS – 4609
RS – 8817
Black Magic – 1379
White Magic – 348
Total – 36,134

1983
Base – 1979
L – 8343

GS – 7080
RS – 6319
Turbo RS – 381
Black Magic – 469
Crimson Cat – 805
Total – 25,376

1984
GS – 15,613
RS – 3648
Turbo RS – 1321
Total – 20,582

1985
GS – 13,785
RS – 4869
Total – 18,654

1986
GS – 17,029
RS – 3840
Total – 20,869

Also from Veloce Publishing –

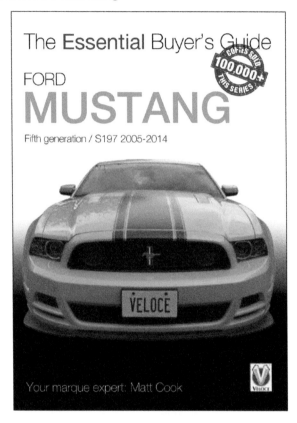

The **Essential** Buyer's Guide

FORD

MUSTANG

Fifth generation / S197 2005-2014

Your marque expert: Matt Cook

Having this book in your pocket is just like having a real marque expert by your side. Benefit from the author's years of Mustang ownership, learn how to spot a bad car quickly, and how to assess a promising car like a professional. Get the right car at the right price!

ISBN: 978-1-845847-98-2
Paperback • 19.5x13.9cm • 64 pages • 108 colour pictures

For more information and price details, visit our website at www.veloce.co.uk
• email: info@veloce.co.uk • Tel: +44(0)1305 260068

Index

Notes